THE
PERFECT COLLECTION

EDITED BY TOM HIBBERT

PROTEUS BOOKS
LONDON AND NEW YORK

PROTEUS BOOKS is an imprint of
The Proteus Publishing Group

United States
PROTEUS PUBLISHING CO., INC.
733 Third Avenue
New York, NY 10017

distributed by
THE SCRIBNER BOOK COMPANIES, INC.
597 Fifth Avenue
New York, NY 10017

PROTEUS (PUBLISHING) LTD
Bremar House
Sale Place
London W2 1PT

ISBN 0 86276 105 0 (paperback)
     0 86276 106 9 (hardback)

First published in UK 1982
First published in US 1982

Copyright © Proteus Publishing 1982

Design **Sharmans**
Editor **Christopher Goodwin**
Typeset by **SX Composing Ltd, Rayleigh, Essex**
Printed by **Printer Industria Grafica sa, Barcelona, Spain**
D. L. B. **29271 – 1982**

Contents

Contributors

A.S. – Andy Schwarz, editor/publisher of 'New York Rocker'

B.H. – Brian Hogg, editor of 'Bam Balam'

B.K. – Bill Knight, editor of 'Prairie Sun' ('The midwest's best rockers . . . by the midwest's best writers')

C.C. – Chris Charlesworth, author of 'The A-Z Of Rock Guitarists'

C.P.L. – C. P. Lee, Alberto Y Lost Trios Paranoias personality and freelance writer

C.W. – Chris Welch, famed rock journalist

F.K. – Fran Kershner, editor of 'Snap It Around'

G.D. – Giovanni Dadomo, fabled pop writer

H.S. – Harry Shapiro, author of 'The A-Z Of Rock Drummers'

I.B. – Ian Birch, reviews editor of 'Smash Hits' and broadcaster

J.T. – John Tobler, legendary rock archivist

K.K. – Kerry King, editor of 'Jelly Jungle'

('All the bubble that's fit to gum!')

M.H. – Michael Heatley, deputy editor of 'The History Of Rock'

M.M. – Mike McDowell, editor/publisher of 'Blitz')'America's fastest growing Rock 'n' Roll magazine!')

M.P. – Martin Plimmer, author of 'The Rock Factory'

M.W. – Mark Williams, greatest living Englishman

N.C. – Nigel Cross, editor of 'Bucketfull Of Brains'

N.W. – Neville Wiggins, punk

P.C. – Peter Clark, editor of E*l P*e books

P.H. – Patrick Humphries, writes for 'Melody Maker'

P.P. – Paddy Poltock, editor of 'Cheesergerburger Chunes'

P.W. – Paul Whitcombe, one man band

S.L. – Stephen Lee, psychologist

S.P. – Sally Payne, distinguished music writer

Some acknowledgements: A gigantic thank you to everyone who contributed (especially as they didn't even get paid) and in particular to Al Clark, Sally Payne, Steve Lee, Andy Childs, Michael Heatley, R. K. Hibbert and Peter Clark. They know what for . . . Bring on the jiving martians . . .

Introduction

'The Perfect Collection' is the kind of book I really hate. Or rather, I should say, it's the type of book I **love** to hate; for nothing gives a boring old pop buff greater perverse pleasure than turning the pages of such a publication and heaping scorn on the editor's choice of great rock records and upon his/her critical analyses of same. 'How can they *possibly* overlook the pioneering work of Teddy and the Pandas on their "seminal" debut concept outing **Basic Magnetism**?' one shrieks with fury, flinging the book to earth. Which only serves to prove that one man's 'perfect collection' is another's aural nightmare: I could never be parted from a copy of **Basic Magnetism** (which, I'm convinced, provides the vital missing link 'twixt the Honeycombs and Joy Division) and yet the album and, in particular, the awesomely squeaky tones of singer Al Lawrence and the cheeky primitivism of Paul Rivers' guitar, leaves many listeners cold (and turns some distinctly queasy).

The collection assembled in this book, then, isn't really perfect at all. I doubt if there's any discerning person in the world who would enjoy sitting through each one of the two hundred plus LPs included (I can't stand some of them myself). And yet the collection would, I trust, be pretty ideal for any wide-boy from Mars wishing to get the history of pop and rock in perspective.

The collection was assembled from the choices of a crack team of music writers and assorted fans whose comments appear beneath each listing. Many of the more idiosyncratic selections have had to be omitted for the sake of balance and sanity; for instance, C. P. Lee and Fran Kershner's choices included **Bobby And Betty Go To The Moon** ('A unique glimpse into the terrifying twin worlds of concept albums and children's parties. Side one charts B & B's rocket trip to the moon – quote: "Gee, this hyper space linear time warp is really swell, Betty" – while on side two it's music and fun all the way at the moon base party. An essential LP that poses the question: "Are session musicians a strong argument for abortion?"',' they commented.) Peter Clark, on the other hand, chose **Memorable Cup Finals** (a record believed to be comprised of nothing but the manic squealing of football commentators) whilst it took considerable restraint on the editor's part to omit Teddy and the Pandas 'seminal' debut concept album ... Many tempered idiocies and a modicum of bias remain, however – this has proved to be unavoidable and, indeed, desirable in order to keep the pulses racing and excitement at fever pitch.

Some contributors entered the foray with enthusiasm – Andy Childs, bless him, compiled a massive list of 253 titles, though he offered no comment apart from: 'The next 253 great albums haven't been made yet.' Others approached the task with a more jaded eye: 'After thumbing my way through my collection, I realised Toe Fat weren't all they're cracked up to be,' admitted Paddy Poltock. 'Just now I'm going through my John Lydon 'all-music-is-shit' period. Who can blame me? I've just seen 'Top Of The Pops'. Would you believe it? Nothing but football songs – not one by Queens Park Rangers! Come on you hoops!' Others again recognised the mighty responsibilities of the job in hand: 'I wonder if the world's rock collections are all going to end up dusty, yellowed, scratched and unglued?' asked Chris Welch. 'This could be a crisis as great as the Nitro film stock disaster.' Indeed. A few instructions: **Labels:** UK label is listed first, US second. **Dates:** These refer to year of original release, though many of the LPs included have been re-issued, re-packed, re-channeled, re-vamped, re-whatever turns the hoary old companies on. **Comments:** These range from snappy one-liners to prolonged and extensive critical investigations. Disparity of opinion between the various contributors has been retained. **Musicians:** Where albums cover a wide range of an artist's career, or where riddled by faceless session musicians, these have, in most cases, been omitted. **Alternative choices:** In certain cases, where an artist or group has made two albums which are similar stylistically and of equal artistic merit, the second is lettered 'a' to denote an alternative choice. **Various artists:** V.A. compilations have, after much debate, been declared ineligible.

TOM HIBBERT

Pre-Sixties/Pre-Pop

. . . Suddenly the children 'twist twelve and twenty had something all their own. To maw and paw, this curious blend of musical styles – hillbilly and country and rock and roll – was simply a rather nasty racket. But to their offspring, it was 'rock 'n' roll' and a jolly sight more exciting than 'The Burns And Allen Show'. Then a sneering, mumbling youth named Elvis Presley appeared on the TV screen with disgusting hair and maw and paw finally saw the new noise for what it was – a celebration of sex and youthful revolt, of self-destructive urges and not-giving-a-damn. But it was too late, for the children had turned into things called 'teenagers' and, with a little help from wily business-men, had begun an irreversible cultural revolution. Oh dear, oh dear, tut-tutted maw and paw as Junior squandered yet another monthly allowance on gramophone records of howling sounds and conversed in a vocabulary ever more baffling. 'Crazy.' 'Dig.' 'Wild.' 'Big Bopper.' What did it all mean? Oh dear, oh dear. Never mind, that Pat Boone seems a nice young man, thought maw as she turned off the front porch light and made her way upstairs . . .

1

Robert Johnson

'King Of The Delta Blues Singers'

Label: **CBS**/Columbia
Date: **1969**

Includes: **Crossroads Blues • Terraplane Blues • Preaching Blues • Walking Blues • Rambling On My Mind • Hellhound On My Trail**

ɪɪNext to nothing is known about the great Robert Johnson. No picture survives. But what we *do* know is that during the thirties, he cut some thirty-odd songs which are among the most harrowing and darkest blues ever recorded. His influence, which extended down to Bob Dylan, the Rolling Stones and Eric Clapton, was immense.**ɪɪ** – **P.H.**

2

Hank Williams

'40 Greatest Hits'

Label: **MGM**/MGM
Date: **1978 (double)**

Includes: **Cold Cold Heart • Howlin' At The Moon • Hey Good Lookin' • You Win Again • I Saw The Light • Move It On Over • Ramblin' Man • Kaw-Liga**

ɪɪIt's pathetic, really, that since Williams popped off in the back of a car on New Years Day 1953, no-one has taken country music any further. It says much about the form that its greatest ever exponent should have been a drunken, drug-oriented, neurotic, helpless sociopath, bent on self-destruction. His emotive nasal whine lives on and makes the mawkish crooning of (nearly) all the rest seem futile.**ɪɪ** – **Ed.**

ɪɪThe first true pop star. Music to herd cows by.**ɪɪ** – **P.P.**

ɪɪThe man who started it all. Without Hank's uncanny honesty and uninhibited delivery, inspiration for future performers would have been severely curtailed.**ɪɪ** – **M.M.**

ɪɪHis plaintive voice and achingly lonely songs are the foundation for all that's best in C&W, through Waylon Jennings, Gram Parsons and Elvis Costello. William's songs were probably the nearest a white man ever came to singing the blues. A vital influence on Bob Dylan and Van Morrison to name but two of his hundreds of disciples.**ɪɪ** – **P.H.**

3

Elvis Presley

'The Sun Collection

Label: **RCA**/RCA
Date: **1975**

Includes: **That's All Right • Blue Moon Of Kentucky • I'm Left, You're Right, She's Gone • Mystery Train • You're A Heartbreaker • Milk Cow Blues Boogie**

ɪɪ*The* rock 'n' roll album. Quintessential Elvis, before 'Colonel' Parker, the Army and Las Vegas sunk their claws in. Raw and threatening, cajoling and tender, as you hear Elvis single-handedly invent rock 'n' roll. Timeless and essential, the music still sounds as powerful today as it did over a quarter of a century ago**ɪɪ** – **P.H.**

ɪɪThe foundation for all that followed.**ɪɪ** – **C.C.**

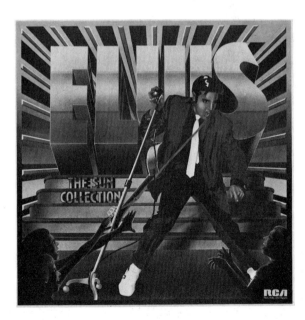

4

Johnny Burnette

'Johnny Burnette And The Rock 'N' Roll Trio'

Label: **MCA/Coral**
Date: **1971**

Includes: **Honey Hush** ● **Lonesome Train** ● **All By Myself** ● **The Train Kept A Rollin'** ● **Drinkin' Wine Spo-Dee-O-Dee**

❪❪Essential rockabilly. Music to flick grease to.❫❫ – **Ed.**

Musicians: **Johnny Burnette** (guitar, vocals) ● **Dorsey Burnette** (bass) ● **Paul Burlison** (guitar)

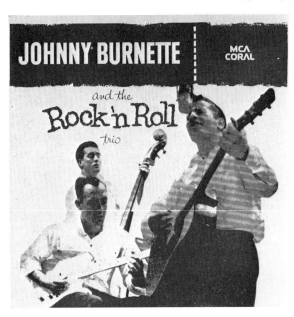

___5___

Chuck Berry

'Motorvatin' '

Label: **Chess/–**
Date: **1976**

Includes: **Johnny B. Goode** ● **Roll Over Beethoven** ● **Maybellene** ● **Bye Bye Johnny** ● **No Particular Place To Go** ● **Sweet Little Sixtgeen** ● **The Promised Land**

❪❪Musically, if not culturally, as influential as Elvis Presley. If Berry received a cent each time a guitarist ripped off his patterns, he'd be an even richer property owner than he is. An observer, a wit, a king guitarist and the writer

of 'The Promised Land' which just about says it all.❫❫ – **Ed.**

___6___

John Lee Hooker

'Dimples'

Label: **DJM/–**
Date: **1977**

Includes: **Wheel And Deal** ● **Mambo Chillum** ● **Baby Lee** ● **Dimples** ● **Boom Boom** ● **I'm So Excited** ● **Maudie** ● **I See You When You're Weak**

❪❪Atmospheric blues and boogie shuffles in a pork pie hat. The perfect antidote for a lost weekend.❫❫ – **S.L.**

___7___

Bo Diddley

'Bo Diddley's Golden Decade'

Label: **Chess/–**
Date: **1973**

Includes: **Bo Diddley** ● **Hey Bo Diddley** ● **Diddley Daddy** ● **I'm A Man** ● **Road Runner** ● **Bo Diddley's A Gunslinger** ● **Who Do You Love**

❪❪For one of the essential beats, for one of the most unashamed vanities, for some of the most ridiculous guitars and for never being a bore.❫❫ – **Ed.**

Jerry Lee Lewis

'The Greatest Live Show On Earth'

Label: **Philips/Smash**
Date: **1964**

Includes: **Jenny Jenny ● High Heel Sneakers ● Memphis ● No Particular Place To Go ● Who Will The Next Fool Be ● Hound Dog**

❪❪The only performer whose enormous ego is superceded by a monstrous talent. This superb live set is more than adequate testimony to the man's right to claim the title of the King of rock and roll.**❫❫** – M.M.

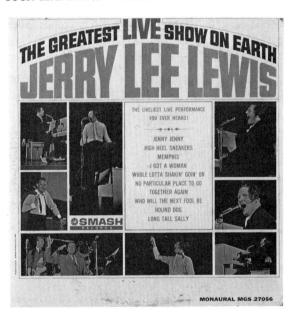

Little Richard

'Good Golly Miss Molly And Eleven Other All-Time Hits'

Label: **Sonet/–**
Date: **1972**

Includes: **Tutti Frutti ● Ready Teddy ● Slippin' And Slidin' ● Good Golly Miss Molly ● Hey Hey Hey Hey ● The Girl Can't Help It ● Lucille**

❪❪The raucous abandoned pounding and whooping of Richard Wayne Penniman highlights the uncompromisingly light and optimistic face of rock 'n' roll**❫❫** – S.L.

❪❪Who's that banging on the piano?**❫❫** – Ed.

Buddy Holly

'The Buddy Holly Story'

Label: **Coral/Coral**
Date: **1960**

Includes: **Peggy Sue ● Every Day ● Rave On ● That'll Be The Day ● Heartbeat ● It Doesn't Matter Anymore ● Oh Boy**

❪❪First proof that spotty little wimps can rock too.**❫❫** – Ed.

Eddie Cochran

'Eddie Cochran: Legendary Masters Series'

Label: **United Artists/United Artists**
Date: **1972 (double)**

Includes: **Skinny Jim ● Jeannie Jeannie Jeannie ● Something Else ● Three Stars ● Summertime Blues ● Milk Cow Blues ● Twenty Flight Rock ● Nervous Breakdown ● C'mon Blues**

❪❪A marvellously unorthodox guitar player. A man who had his finger on the pulse of adolescent obsessional problems. A man of influence and verve.**❫❫** – Ed.

12

Gene Vincent

'Gene Vincent's Greatest'

Label: Capitol/Capitol
Date: 1974

Includes: **Be-Bop-A-Lula** • **Who Slapped John** • **Bluejean Bop** • **Jump Back Honey** • **B-I-Bickey-Bi-Bo-Bo-Boo** • **She-She Little Sheila** • **Wild Cat**

ʬWhat a star. The man gave hope to misfits and cripples (social and physical) everywhere. Potent atonal bawling and whining as the squeal of the unacceptable penetrates the greasy barriers of rock 'n' roll music in horrid golf jerseys and black leather. Limping.ʭ – **Ed.**

13

The Coasters

'Coasters Greatest Hits'

Label: London/Atco
Date: 1960

Includes: **Poison Ivy** • **Along Came Jones** • I'm A Hog For You • **Charlie Brown** • **Yakety Yak** • **Young Blood**

ʬWry satire and aural slapstick from the first bunch to truly exploit the esential stupidity of rock 'n' roll and youth sub-cultures.ʭ – S.L.

Musicians: **Billy Guy** • **Carl Gardner** • **Dub Jones** • **Bobby Nunn**

14

Ricky Nelson

'Ricky Sings Again'

Label: London/Imperial
Date: 1958

Includes: **It's Late** • **Believe What You Say** • **Never Be Anyone Else But You** • **You Tear Me Up** • **Restless Kid**

ʬThe most honest and unaffected voice in rock's diverse history in his shining moment. A taste of great things to come.ʭ – M.M.

Musicians: **Ricky Nelson** (vocals) • With: **James Burton** (guitar) • **Joe Osborn** (bass) • **Gene Garth** (keyboards) • **Richie Frost** (drums) • and others

15

The Everly Brothers

'Songs Our Daddy Taught Us'

Label: London/Cadence
Date: 1959

Includes: **Roving Gambler** • **Lightning Express** • **Who's Gonna Shoe Your Pretty Little Feet** • **I'm Here To Get My Baby Out Of Jail** • **Rockin' Along In An Old Rockin' Chair** • **Kentucky**

ʬTheir distinctive close-harmony whining, ever accurate and perfectly phrased, has been as influential on the development of pure pop music as anything else you might care to suggest. Here Don and Phil are heard touting their hillbilly and country influences to tingling effect.ʭ – Ed.

Musicians: **Phil** (the high bits) • **Don** (the low bits)

16

Cliff Richard

'Cliff Sings'

Label: **Columbia/ABC Paramount**
Date: **1959**

Includes: **Blue Suede Shoes** • **Twenty Flight Rock** • **Pointed Toe Shoes** • **I'm Walkin'** • **The Snake And The Bookworm** • **The Touch Of Your Lips**

❝Cliff's Elvis-styled sneer threatens to crack his entire face on this prime example of Britain's boast 'Anything Yanks can do, we can do better (well, almost anyway)'.❞ – **Ed.**

18

Billy Fury

'The Sound Of Fury'

Label: **Decca**/–
Date: **1960**

Includes: **That's Love** • **Phone Call** • **Turn My Back On You** • **Don't Say It's Over** • **It's Yŏu I Need** • **Don't Leave Me This Way**

❝Britain's closest approximation of rocking Elvis makes the first English rockabilly album before turning to mawkish crooning. Joe Brown's no Scotty Moore but that's part of the charm.❞ – **Ed.**

Musicians: **Joe Brown** (guitar) • **Alan Weighell** (bass) • **Reg Guest** (piano) • **Bill Stark** (bass) • **Andy White** (drums)

18

Pat Boone

'22 Original Hits'

Label: **Warwick**/–
Date: **1980**

Includes: **I Almost Lost My Mind** • **Love Letters In The Sand** • **A Wonderful Time Up There** • **Ain't That A Shame** • **Twixt Twelve And Twenty** • **Speedy Gonzales**

❝Pat Boone – he of the lofty moral standards and fundamentalist beliefs – offered teenagers a safer version of the rock rhythms purveyed by Little Richard, Chuck Berry et al. Outsold, during the fifties, by Elvis alone, this great anti-rebel helped to make rock 'n' roll acceptable throughout America. Hence, no Pat – no Beatles. Q.E.D.❞ – **Ed.**

❝For his stand on heavy petting and like perversions. Great Coogamooga! Pat's OK!❞ – **G.D.**

The Sixties: Pre-Beat, Motown and Soul

By 1960, rock 'n' roll had gone into early retirement. Elvis emerged from the army, the laundering and sanitisation process complete, and, following his example, all others began scrubbing away, erasing threatening patches and turning rock safe and clean. The early sixties became an era of instant, disposable pop heard, at its worst, in the pure unexcitement of the Philly teen idols – Fabian, Frankie Avalon et al – and, at its best, in the many fads and crazes that sprouted and withered at alarming speed. This was the age of the dance craze – twist! pony! shake! go! This was the age of girl group pop – Shirelles and Shangs, Chiffons and tons of sobs. This was the age of twang, pioneered by Duane and transmuted to surf by Dick Dale as a rumbling celebration of California sun/fun that the Beach Boys would soon put into words. Then there was Detroit where R&B rhythms turned pop gold in the hands of a small team of master craftsmen. It was the best of times, it was the worst of times. As someone once said . . .

19

Elvis Presley

'Blue Hawaii'

Label: **RCA Victor/RCA Victor**
Date: **1961**

Includes: **Blue Hawaii • Can't Help Falling In Love • Rock-A-Hula Baby • Moonlight Swim • Ku-u-i-po • Slicin' Sand • Hawaiian Wedding Song**

ſſPurists and archivists sweat with horror at anything the so-called king did after the army. They excuse Elvis for this imagined fall from artistic grace by blaming the Colonel. Perhaps they're right. Who cares? This is an extremely silly pop album, admittedly, but it also happens to be one of the most enjoyable artefacts of the early sixties. And it *also* happens to be Elvis' best-selling LP of all time. Ku-u-i-po, let's GO!**JJ** – **Ed.**

19a

Elvis Presley

'Girls! Girls! Girls!'

Label: **RCA Victor/RCA Victor**
Date: **1962**

Includes: **Girls! Girls! Girls! • I Don't Wanna Be Tied • Earth Boy • Return To Sender • Song Of The Shrimp • We're Coming In Loaded**

ſſA classic soundtrack album from one of the most flimsy films ever committed to celluloid. Not only do the songs include Elvis' finest pop moment, in 'Return To Sender', they contain a message for the future in 'We're Coming In Loaded' – get it? The movie is a sailor boy yarn – Elvis' way of saying 'Look, fellas, we're all in the same boat.' He was not to be heeded, as the horror history shows. **JJ** – **Ed.**

20

Cliff Richard

'Me And My Shadows'

Label: **Columbia/–**
Date: **1960**

Includes: **Evergreen Trees • She's Gone • Lamp Of Love • Gee Whiz Tell Me It's You • I Love You So • I Don't Know • You And I**

ſſCliff returns from army service (surely some mistake here?) and mellows into moody teen idol with a batch of digestibles. But, gee whiz! Can the boy sing!**JJ** – **Ed.**

Musicians: **Cliff** • With: **The Shadows** – **Jet Harris** (bass) • **Hank B. Marvin** (guitar) • **Bruce Welch** (guitar) • **Tony Meehan** (drums)

21

Chubby Checker

'For Twisters Only'

Label: **Columbia/Parkway**
Date: **1962**

Includes: **Hound Dog • Twist Train • Mister Twister • But Girls! • Dance With Me Henry • At The Hop • Hound Dog • Shake Rattle And Roll • Rock Around The Clock**

ſſOle Chubs twists up a storm, whooping his way through a feast of rock 'n' roll classics, all wound up to suit his ridiculous style. Is that a bird? . . . No! . . . Is that a plane? . . . No! . . . It's jus' tubby old Ernest Evans pioneering a partnerless dance craze. Twisterrificcc!!!**JJ** – **Ed.**

22

Duane Eddy

'Legend Of Rock'

Label: **London/–**
Date: **1974**

Includes: **Because They're Young • Ramrod • Shazam! • Forty Miles Of Bad Road • Some Kinda Earthquake**

❞ A deep, cavernous guitar boom, rebel whoops and hysterical sax spell the birth of instrumental rock, for better or worse. Have Gretsch will travel for, as any fool knows, the twang's the thang. **❞** – Ed.

23

The Surfaris
'Fun City, U.S.A.'

Label: **Brunswick/Decca**
Date: **1963**

Includes: **Dune Buggy • Hot Rod Graveyard • Murphy The Surfie • Hot Rod High • Moon Dawg • Go Go Go For Louie's Place • Burnin' Rubber**

❞ Probably the best of the US surfing instrumentalists on probably their best LP. Where the Ventures were weedy and the Chantays inconsistent and non-prolific, the Surfaris kept their woodys afloat for months. Just listen to the guitar tone, on 'Moon Dawg' in particular, and re-evaluate your punk-axe ideology. **❞** – Ed.

Musicians: **Pat Connolly** (vocals, bass) • **Jim**

Fuller (guitar) • **Bob Berryhill** (guitar) • **Ron Wilson** (drums) • **Jim Pash** (sax)

24

The Beach Boys
'Best Of The Beach Boys'

Label: **Capitol/Capitol**
Date: **1966**

Includes: **Surfin' Safari • Fun Fun Fun • I Get Around • Help Me Rhonda • California Girls • Barbara Ann • Sloop John B • God Only Knows**

❞ Affable, young Americans celebrate the realised dream of the Golden state – eternal sun-kiss, wheels and water-sports, and girls who are never ugly. Bags o' fun (until, that is, daddy takes the T-Bird away). **❞** – Ed.

Musicians: **Brian Wilson • Dennis Wilson • Carl Wilson • Mike Love • Al Jardine • David Marks**

25

Annette
'Muscle Beach Party'

Label: **–/Buena Vista**
Date: **1964**

Includes: **Custom City • Draggin' USA • Shut Down Again • Waikiki • Muscle Beach Party**

[[Ex-Mouseketeer Annette Funicello may have possessed one of the thinnest, most insubstantial voices in the history of popular music, but when it came to a corny beach party anthem the beauty's tones were unbeatable. On this album, her naïve yet enthusiastic breezing combines with the thin exuberance of Gary Usher, Brian Wilson and Roger Christian's songs to produce THE surf/beach/drag classic of endless summer. Also the most thrilling cover of all time.**]]** – **Ed.**

…ean

Label: …ty/Liberty

…s

…es: **The Universal Coward** ● **Turn Turn …n** ● **Eve Of Destruction**

[[A rare case where a performer can defy a stereotype and succeed both spiritually and aesthetically.**]]** – **M.M.**

Musicians: **Jan Berry** ● **Dean Torrence** ● plus support

27

Del Shannon

'20 Golden Greats'

Label: **EMI**/ –

Date: **1978**

Includes: **Hats Off To Larry** ● **Runaway** ● **The Swiss Maid** ● **Pretty Woman** ● **Little Town Flirt**

[[In an age of laundered teen idols, Del remained his own man. Raucous pop for disaffected carpet salesmen and Maximillian's organ is truly inspired.**]]** – **Ed.**

28

Shangri-Las

'Golden Hits'

Label: **Philips/Mercury**
Date: **1973**

Includes: **Remember (Walking In The Sand)** ● **Leader Of The Pack** ● **I Can Never Go Home Anymore** ● **Give Him A Great Big Kiss** ● **Past Present And Future** ● **Give Us Your Blessings**

[[The Shangri-Las were to the mid-sixties what Trevor Howard and Celia Johnson in 'Brief Encounter' had been to the late forties – heart-wrenching self-pity/sacrifice and not a dry eye in the house. The Shangs were ever in the thick of it; loved ones/parents/themselves would die due to misunderstandings/lost romance in the most finely produced (by George 'Shadow' Morton) teen anthem/melodramas of the decade (and that includes Phil Spector). But were the girls ruffled? Well, yes, most of the time – but they still bounced back, on occasion, to 'give him a great big kiss

. . . mooooIIII!' Quintessential white girl-group rock and quite indispensable. **JJ** – **Ed.**

Musicians: **Betty Weiss • Mary Weiss • Margie Ganser • Mary Ann Ganser**

29

The Ronettes

'Presenting The Fabulous Ronettes Featuring Veronica'

Label: –/Philles
Date: 1964

Includes: **Be My Baby/Baby I Love You/ Breakin' Up/Chapel Of Love/You Baby/Do I Love You**

ffThe best example of the craft of so-called eccentric genius Phil Spector's production techniques. At their blustering finest, atop the semi-legendary wall of sound, the fab Ronettes could move mountains. Ronnie's 'woah-woah-woahs' remain amongst the most titillating vocal moments of the sixties or any other decade. **JJ** – **Ed.**

Musicians: **Veronica Bennett (Ronnie Spector) • Estelle Bennett • Nedra Talley**

30

Dusty Springfield

'Dusty Springfield's Golden Hits'

Label: **Philips/Philips**
Date: **1968**

Includes: **You Don't Have To Say You Love Me • Losing You • Little By Little • I Only Want To Be With You • I Just Don't Know What To Do With Myself**

ffWhat a croak in the throat meant in the early sixties! **JJ** – **I.B.**

31

Sam Cooke

'The Golden Age Of Sam Cooke'

Label: **RCA/–**
Date: **1976**

Includes: **Chain Gang • Wonderful World • Bring It On Home To Me • A Change Is Gonna Come • Another Saturday Night**

ffThe first great soul solo singer to reach white audiences. His songs have been covered by everyone from the Animals to Rod Stewart to Ry Cooder to Herman's Hermits, but the originals are still the best. If he hadn't died when he did, shot in a sordid near-rape, then he would probably have become Frank Sinatra. He would never have turned into Perry Como. **JJ** – **S.L.**

32

Otis Redding

'Otis Blue'

Label: **Atlantic/Volt**
Date: **1966**

Includes: **Respect • I've Been Loving You Too Long • My Girl • Ole Man Trouble • You Don't Miss Your Water**

ffIf ever a performer epitomised 'soul', it was Otis Redding. His death in 1967 was a catastrophic loss from which the world of music has never recovered. **JJ** – **M.M.**

33

Aretha Franklin

'Ten Years Of Gold'

Label: **Atlantic/Atlantic**
Date: 1976

Includes: **Respect ● A Natural Woman ● Spanish Harlem ● Baby I Love You ● Think ● I Never Loved A Man (The Way I Love You)**

❝Stand up, loosen up and dance to the most consistently exciting female voice to have emerged from American soul. Eat your heart out Toyah.**❞** – C.P.L. & F.K.

34

The Contours

'Baby Hit And Run'

Label: **MFP/–**
Date: 1976

Includes: **Just A Little Misunderstanding ● First I Look At The Purse ● Can You Jerk Like Me ● Baby Hit And Run ● Can You Do It ● Do You Love Me?**

❝The essence of hard Motown R&B/soul music. This really is it; growling dance music that sparked off a gaggle of pretenders. 'Can You Jerk Like Me' must be the most stirring dance record ever to emerge from the automobile city. Hoarse and irresistible.**❞** – Ed.

Musicians: **Billy Gordon ● Sylvester Potts ● Joe Billingslea ● Billy Hoggs ● Hubert Johnson ● Huey Davis ● Dennis Edwards**

35

Smokey Robinson And The Miracles

'Anthology'

Label: **Tamla Motown/Tamla Motown**
Date: 1974 (triple)

Includes: **Shop Around ● You've Really Got A Hold On Me ● Mickey's Monkey ● The Tracks Of My Tears ● Going To A Go-Go ● I Second That Emotion ● Tears Of A Clown**

❝Astonishing in its musical breadth, vocal artistry and lyric poetry.**❞** – A.S.

Musicians: **Smokey Robinson ● Claudette Rogers ● Bobby Rogers ● Ronni White ● Warren Moore ● Marvin Tarplin ●** and others

36

The Temptations

'The Temptations Sing Smokey'

Label: **Tamla Motown/Gordy**
Date: 1965

Includes: **You've Really Got A Hold On Me ● You Beat Me To The Punch ● The Way You Do The Things You Do ● My Girl ● It's Growing**

❝Simply beautiful. A combination of those marvellous harmonies singing the best of Smokey Robinson can be little else. What makes this record so perfect is the care – each song is treated as would be a single, tenderly arranged to suit those voices. **❞** – B.H.

Musicians: **Eddie Kendricks** ● **David Ruffin** ● **Otis Miles** ● **Melvin Franklin** ● **Paul Williams**

37

The Four Tops

'Greatest Hits'

Label: **Tamla Motown/Motown**
Date: **1968**

Includes: **Reach Out I'll Be There** ● **Standing In The Shadows Of Love** ● **Bernadette** ● **Seven Rooms Of Gloom** ● **Baby I Need Your Loving** ● **It's The Same Old Song**

❝Masters of the three-minute soul single present a collection of their finest vinyl – play it loud and you've got an instant party. The combination of Levi Stubbs' voice and the compositions of Holland-Dozier-Holland make these Motown at its most memorable. **❞** – M.H.

Musicians: **Levi Stubbs** ● **Renaldo Benson** ● **Lawrence Payton** ● **Abdul Fakir**

38

Diana Ross And The Supremes

'Greatest Hits'

Label: **Tamla Motown/Motown**
Date: **1967**

Includes: **Stop! In The Name Of Love** ● **Where Did Our Love Go** ● **Come See About Me** ● **Reflections** ● **Back In My Arms Again** ● **You Keep Me Hanging On** ● **Baby Love**

❝The husky tones of Diana Ross before she joined the snivelling jet-set, the chirpy support of Mary Wilson and Florence Ballard, the instinctive commercial flair of Holland-Dozier-Holland, the Motown sound, the tambourines, and 'there ain't nothin' you can do about it', etc. **❞** – Ed.

Musicians: **Diana Ross** ● **Mary Wilson** ● **Florence Ballard** ● and a supporting cast of thousands

39

Marvin Gaye

'The Best Of Marvin Gaye'

Label: **Motown/Motown**
Date: **1976**

Includes: **I Heard It Through The Grapevine** •
Too Busy Thinking About My Baby • **That's
The Way Love Is** • **Let's Get It On You Sure
Love To Ball** • **Save The Children**

❛❛Ten years of sweet soul music that touches
all corners of emotion.**❜❜** – S.L.

Mid-Sixties/UK

"Dear John, Although all the Beatles are 'fab' in every way and form, you are the 'fabbiest' of them all. I love you, John so much that I bought you this cuddly toy, which is what I think of you as. Perhaps you would give it to your baby." – Letter from fan to John Lennon, 1964.

"The whole lot of you should be given a good bath and then all that hair should be cut off. I'm not against pop music when it's performed by a nice clean boy like Cliff Richard but you are a disgrace. Your filthy appearance is liable to corrupt teenagers all over the country." – Letter from parent to Rolling Stones, 1964.

The Empire strikes back. By 1965, the Liverpool beat and the R&B boom centred around London had usurped America's domination of youth culture, paving the way for the march of the mods and Herman's weeny-pop brigade. On February 9th, 1964, the Beatles arrived at the CBS studios on New York's 53rd Street to rehearse for their appearance on the 'Ed Sullivan Show'. Outside, a young man strolled bearing a placard that read: 'Alonzo Tuske Hates The Beatles'. But Alonzo's was a lone voice, whistling down the wind...

40

The Beatles

'With The Beatles'

Label: **Parlophone**/–
Date: 1963

Includes: **All My Loving** ● **All I've Got To Do** ●
It Won't Be Long ● **Please Mister Postman** ●
You Really Got A Hold On Me ● **Money**

《 For me, the perfect Beatle album, completely consolidating the group's individuality and
importance. It combines their ever-growing
original songs – rocking 'It Won't Be Long', the
commercial 'All My Loving', the driving 'Not A
Second Time' – with more of the Cavern stage
favourites: 'Money', 'Roll Over Beethoven' and
'Please Mr Postman'. It's unhesitating music,
amply proving the Beatles as leaders **》** – **B.H.**

Musicians: **The Fab Four**

41

The Rolling Stones

'The Rolling Stones'

Label: **Decca/London**
Date: 1964

Includes: **Route 66** ● **I Just Want To Make Love
To You** ● **I Need You Baby** ● **Little By Little** ●
I'm A King Bee ● **Can I Get A Witness**

《 There are few debut albums which can
claim such self-confidence and assuredness.
The Rolling Stones simply ooze power, pounding their way through such classic R&B standards as Chuck Berry's 'Carol', Willie Dixon's 'I
Just Want To Make Love To You' and Holland,
Dozier and Holland's 'Can I Get A Witness'.
The Rolling Stones is the definitive British R&B
collection and, of course, the beginning of a
fascinating career. **》** – **B.H.**

Musicians: **Mick Jagger** (vocals) ● **Keith
Richard** (guitar) ● **Brian Jones** (guitar) ● **Bill
Wyman** (bass) ● **Charlie Watts** (drums)

42

Yardbirds

'Five Live Yardbirds'

Label: **Columbia**/–
Date: 1965

Includes: **I Got Love If You Want It** ●
Smokestack Lightning ● **Good-morning Little
Schoolgirl** ● **Louise** ● **I'm A Man** ● **Here 'Tis**

《 *Five Live Yardbirds* corresponds directly
with *The Rolling Stones,* being British R&B's
definitive *live* album. The group are perfect
within this performance context (its recorded
during their 1964 Marquee residency) and
combine blues standards – the superlative
'Smokestack Lightning', 'Here 'Tis', 'I'm A Man'
and more – with a new instrumental preoc-

cupation which paved the way for much of the late sixties rock. Eric Clapton is simply excellent JJ – B.H.

Musicians: **Keith Relf** (vocals) ● **Eric Clapton** (guitar) ● **Paul Samwell-Smith** (bass) ● **Jim McCarty** (drums) ● **Chris Dreja** (Guitar)

43

Manfred Mann

'Five Faces Of Manfred Mann'

Label: **HMV/Ascot**
Date: **1964**

Includes: **Smokestack Lightning** ● **Sack O'Woe** ● **What You Gonna Do** ● **Mr Anello** ● **Untie Me** ● **Bring It To Jerome** ● **Hoochie Coochie**

JJWhereas so much of British R&B was fast and furious, Manfred Mann's first offered a real alternative with a measured, reflective approach, replacing rawness with care. The group show their jazz roots with saxophones or vibes replacing the expected guitar solos. They also rearrange the songs, giving them freshness, and attempt at building originality through this approach which is mirrored within their own compositions. A marvellous and distinctive album. JJ – B.H.

Musicians: **Manfred Mann** (keyboards) ● **Paul Jones** (vocals) ● **Tom McGuinness** (bass, guitar) ● **Mike Vickers** (sax) ● **Mike Hugg** (drums)

44

The Spencer Davis Group

'The Second Album'

Label: **Fontana/–**
Date: **1966**

Includes: **Keep On Running** ● **Look Away** ● **Strong Love** ● **Let Me Down Easy** ● **I Washed My Hands In Muddy Water** ● **Hey Darling**

JJStevie Winwood at his teenaged best on

vocals, guitars, keyboards and inspiration. JJ – C.W.

Musicians: **Spencer Davis** (guitar, vocals) ● **Muff Winwood** (bass, vocals) ● **Steve Winwood** (guitar, keyboards, vocals) ● **Pete York** (drums)

45

The Animals

'Animalisms'

Label: **Decca/MGM**
Date: **1966**

Includes: **One Monkey Don't Stop No Show** ● **Sweet Little Sixteen** ● **Gin House Blues** ● **What Am I Living For** ● **I Put A Spell On You** ● **That's All I Am To You**

JJIn many ways, *Animalisms* is the last great British R&B album. By now, most of the group's contemporaries were recording original material but this is an uncompromising collection of Animals stage favourites alongside the very occasional original (of which 'Outcast' is especially good). It was sadly anachronistic – the group split soon after its release – but it remains a strong, mature album and a fine ending and summation of an era. JJ – B.H.

Musicians: **Eric Burdon** (vocals) ● **Hilton Valentine** (guitar) ● **Chas Chandler** (bass) ● **John Steel** (drums) ● **Dave Rowberry** (keyboards)

46

The Kinks

'Something Else'

Label: **Pye/Reprise**
Date: **1967**

Includes: **David Watts** ● **Death Of A Clown** ● **Harry Rag** ● **Tin Soldier Man** ● **Love Me Till The Sun Shines** ● **Afternoon** ● **Waterloo Sunset**

JJIf there ever existed, within the instant, disposable genre of pop music, anyone with a plausible claim to the over-worked title 'Genius', Raymond Douglas Davies was it. Lennon, McCartney, Spector et al, all had their wonky moments but, during the sixties, Davies never put a foot, a note or a word wrong. The Kinks were one of the very few groups of the era to devote equal effort to producing albums as they did to singles – they never cut anything approaching 'filler' material. On this, their fifth official LP, Davies' immaculate songwriting skill reaches a peak of maturity.**)) – Ed.**

((_Something Else_ completely confirms the Kinks' own self-determination; making no concession to their own contemporary environment, the album simply progresses within the group's own music. It's pure England – from the rhyming slang of 'Harry Rag', the hope of 'Situation Vacant', the imagery of 'Two Sisters' and the superb drive of the schoolboy hero anthem 'David Watts'. The album represents the Kinks', and Ray Davies', crowning achievement**)) – B.H.**

Musicians: **Ray Davies** (vocals, guitar) ● **Dave Davies** (vocals, guitar) ● **Pete Quaife** (bass) ● **Mick Avory** (drums)

47

The Beatles

'Rubber Soul'

Label: **Parlophone/Capital**
Date: 1965

Includes: **Drive My Car** ● **Norwegian Wood** ● **Nowhere Man** ● **Girl** ● **I'm Looking Through You** ● **In My Life**

((The crucial link between Beatlemania and the acid excesses of _Sergeant Pepper, Rubber Soul_ is the most durable Beatles album, lyrically and musically. It shows them comfortable and willing to experiment in the studio, but never straying too far from the perfect three minute pop song. It's not just a question of a 'favourite' Beatles album, _Rubber Soul_ could be played to someone who had never heard of the most fabled pop group in history and it would still stand on its own merits.**)) – P.H.**

Musicians: **J●P●G●R**

47a

The Beatles

'Revolver'

Label: **Parlophone/Capitol**
Date: 1966

Includes: **Eleanor Rigby** ● **Taxman** ● **She Said She Said** ● **Good Day Sunshine** ● **Doctor Robert** ● **Tomorrow Never Knows**

((Everyone's had their two penneth worth. Just good damn songs, everyone. Could help fill up the gaps in your mind.**)) – P.P.**

Musicians: **Johnny and the Moondogs?**

48

The Yardbirds

'Yardbirds'

Label: **Columbia/–**
Date: **1966**

Includes: **Over Under Sideways Down** ● **Nazz Are Blue** ● **Rack My Mind** ● **Farewell** ● **Hot House Of Omagarashid** ● **Jeff's Boogie** ● **Turn Into Earth**

❝An early glimpse of English psychedelia as Jeff Beck, far and away the most imaginative guitarist of the era, strives to boldly go (electronically speaking) where no man has gone before. His boring jazz-oriented preoccupations of the following decade cannot detract from this statement of his art.❞ – **Ed.**

❝One of the most exciting and talented UK bands of the early/mid-sixties. What Jeff Beck does to his guitar still amazes to this day.❞ – **N.C.**

❝R&B is transformed into 'pop art' as the Yardbirds spearhead a new progressive British pop. Crammed with experiment and new ideas, as well as fine songs, the album represents the real growth of UK sixties music from its outright derivation of rhythm and blues to a new, independent and vital form of its own.❞ – **B.H.**

Musicians: **Keith Relf** (vocals) ● **Jeff Beck** (guitar) ● **Chris Dreja** (guitar) ● **Paul Samwell-Smith** (bass) ● **Jim McCarty** (drums)

49

The Who

'My Generation'

Label: **Brunswick/–**
Date: **1965**

Includes: **Out In The Street** ● **The Good's Gone** ● **La La La Lies** ● **My Generation** ● **The Kids Are Alright** ● **It's Not True**

'The Who Sings My Generation'

Label: **– /Decca**
Date: **1965**

Includes: Same as UK version but **Instant Party** replaces **I'm A Man** and **The Kids Are Alright** is edited

❝The Who's debut album and their best by miles and miles and miles. Golden moments of mod/pop-art music refined to perfection and Townshend's stunning use of power-chord solos is a lesson in innovation. This is the perfect power-pop statement and it's a tragedy that big-nosed Pete forgot his own teachings.❞ – **Ed.**

❝The Who made two attempts at recording a debut album: the first contained mostly cover versions, whilst this, the issued alternative, is nearly all Pete Townshend songs. Each is tight and hard, fully achieving the newness and promise the Who's music had already claimed.❞ – **B.H.**

❝The best record Mose Allison ever made.❞ – **G.D.**

Musicians: **Pete Townshend** (guitar) ● **Roger Daltry** (vocals) ● **John Entwhistle** (bass) ● **Keith Moon** (drums)

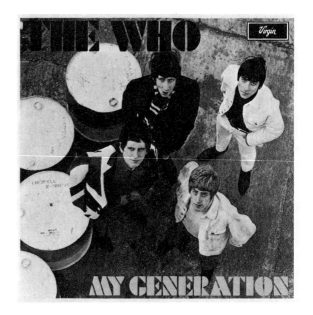

49a

The Who

'Meaty, Beaty, Big And Bouncy'

Label: **Track/Decca**
Date: **1971**

Includes: **I Can't Explain** ● **Happy Jack** ● **I Can See For Miles** ● **Pictures Of Lily** ● **My Generation** ● **Anyway Anyhow Anywhere** ● **Substitute**

❝The best collection of singles from the best British rock group.❞ – **C.C.**

Musicians: **Pete Townshend** (guitar) ● **Roger Daltrey** (vocals) ● **John Entwhistle** (bass) ● **Keith Moon** (drums)

50

The Small Faces

'Small Faces'

Label: **Decca**/–
Date: **1966**

Includes: **Shake** ● **You Better Believe It** ● **Whatcha Gonna Do 'Bout It** ● **Sorry She's Mine** ● **Own Up** ● **Sha La La La Lee**

❛❛A fascinating album showing how much the real heart of the group was hidden behind their singles. Two of the hits are here, 'Whatcha Gonna Do 'Bout It' and 'Sha La La La Lee', and most of the rest either equals or surpasses these. There's an excellent version of 'Shake' and 'E To D'. *Small Faces* is exciting, soul-based pop and, freed from chart preconceptions, shows just how strong the group were in their early days.❜❜ – **B.H.**

Musicians: **Steve Marriott** (vocals, guitar) ● **Ronnie 'Plonk' Lane** (bass) ● **Ian McClagen** (keyboards) ● **Kenny Jones** (drums) ● **Jimmy Winston** (keyboards)

51

Geno Washington And The Ram Jam Band

'Hand Clappin', Foot Stompin', Funky-Butt...Live!'

Label: **Piccadilly**/–
Date: **1966**

Includes: **Land Of 1,000 Dances** ● **Ride Your Pony** ● **Respect** ● **Philly Dog** ● **Road Runner** ● **Hold On I'm Coming**

❛❛Simply the sweatiest album ever. All thrills, no frills; hysterical versions of soul standards segued together and wild audience participation to bring the frenzy into the living room. 'Land Of A Thousand Dances', though speeded up, spills over from side one to side two in ridiculous fashion.❜❜ – **M.P.**

52

The Troggs

'From Nowhere'

Label: **Fontana**/–
Date: **1966**

Includes: **Wild Thing** ● **Evil** ● **Louie Louie** ● **Jingle Jangle** ● **From Home** ● **Jaguar And The Thunderbird**

❛❛Probably the only punk group Britain ever produced. Blundering rhythm guitar and spluttering lead, boom-boom, and, of course, the lame-brained nasal whine of Reg Presley. Brilliant.❜❜ – **Ed.**

Musicians: **Reg Presley** (vocals) ● **Ronnie Bond** (drums) ● **Pete Staples** (bass) ● **Chris Britton** (guitar)

53

Dave Dee, Dozy, Beaky, Mick & Tich

'If Music Be The Food Of Love...'

Label: **Fontana**/–
Date: **1966**

Includes: **Bang** ● **Hideaway** ● **Loos Of England** ● **Master Llewellyn** ● **All I Want** ● **Hair On My Chinny, Chin, Chin (Huff 'N' Puff)** ● **Bend It**

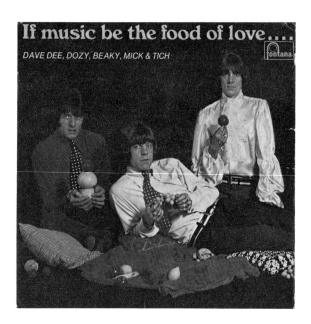

If music be the food of love....
DAVE DEE, DOZY, BEAKY, MICK & TICH

❝Whilst all around were getting 'serious', with psychedelic flirtations and studio explorations, DD, D, B, M & T kept the flag of naïve, innocent pop corn flying high. The one concession to new tendencies is Tich's pathetically fuzz-toned guitar work which buzzes throughout the LP, making 'If Music . . .' the nearest the group ever came to creating a concept album. Thank god they didn't; I could

Musicians: **Dave Dee (David Harman)** (vocals) ● **Ian Amey (Tich)** (guitar) ● **John Dymond (Beaky)** (guitar) ● **Trevor Davies (Dozy)** (bass) ● **Mick Wilson** (drums)

54

Herman's Hermits

'Blaze'

Label: –/MGM
Date: 1967

Includes: **Museum** ● **Busy Line** ● **One Little Packet Of Cigarettes** ● **Last Bus Home** ● **Ace, King, Queen, Jack** ● **Upstairs, Downstars**

❝If ever a band was perceptive enough to perform their autobiography, 'Blaze' shines as the best example. The rhythm section of Green, Leckenby and Whitwam soars throughout the recording.❞ – M.M.

Musicians: **Peter Noone (Herman)** (vocals) ● **Keith Hopwood** (guitar) ● **Derek Leckenby**

(guitar) ● **Karl Green** (bass) ● **Barry Whitwam** (drums)

55

The Easybeats

'Good Friday' (US title: 'Friday On My Mind')

Label: **United Artists/United Artists**
Date: **1967**

Includes: **River Deep, Mountain High** ● **Do You Have A Soul** ● **Friday On My Mind** ● **Happy Is The Man** ● **Made My Bed Gonna Lie In It**

❝Working class power-pop from Australia. Ringing guitars, abrasive pace, energy amidst prevailing introspection, and the commercial rock 'n' roll songs of Vanda and Young. What more could one want from a band who were honest enough to admit they were incapable of making the expected cross from rock to flowery stuff? Whilst most of their contemporaries tripped gaily about in the meadows, the Easybeats were proud to snarl 'We're gonna have fun in the CITY!❞ – Ed.

Musicians: **Harry Vanda** (vocals, guitar) ● **George Young** (vocals, guitar) ● **Steve Wright** (vocals) ● **Dick Diamonde** (bass) ● **Tony Cahill** (drums)

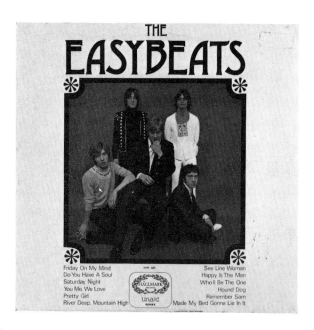

THE **EASYBEATS**

Friday On My Mind
Do You Have A Soul
Saturday Night
You Me We Love
Pretty Girl
River Deep. Mountain High

See Line Woman
Happy Is The Man
Who'll Be The One
Hound Dog
Remember Sam
Made My Bed Gonna Lie In It

The Move

'The Move'

Label: **Regal Zonophone/ –**
Date: **1968**

Includes: **(Here We Go Round) The Lemon Tree** • **Walk Upon The Water** • **Flowers In The Rain** • **Fire Brigade** • **Cherry Blossom Clinic**

❝From mod and auto-destruction, through flower-power and acid rock, to the heavy-handed string and wind concepts (that would, eventually, become ELO), the Move always seemed a trifle restless, musically speaking. But on this, their first album, they are at their very best – loud commercial pop music, courtesy of the best songs that the once multi-talented Roy Wood ever wrote.❞ – **Ed.**

Musicians: **Roy Wood** (vocals, guitar) • **Chris 'Ace' Kefford** (bass) • **Carl Wayne** (vocals) • **Trevor Burton** (guitar) • **Bev Bevan** (drums)

Mid-Sixties/US

"We hate fourteen year old girls from the Bronx who go to the mod shops and say 'What can we get that's English to walk around the Village in today?' And at eleven they have to take off their John Lennon hats and go home." – Victor 'Moulty' Molten, one-handed drummer of New England beat group the Barbarians, 1966.

The Beatles and the Stones had brought a raging wave of Anglophilia to the States and a host of hopefuls skulked around the garages of America, twanging their electric guitars and refining their English accents. Their efforts were, in the main, wasted but the Brit interpretations of a handful – the Beau Brummels, the Knickerbockers, Count Five and others – held an energetic edge that captured the imagination and offered new alternatives. Almost by accident, a unique and novel sound was being forged – the sound of punk. Elsewhere, the traditions of California pop were kept alive by the Beach Boys, the Mamas And The Papas and the Turtles, while others, whose roots lay in folk music were inspired by the British beat to blend the forms and create something else again – folk-rock. Whilst business moguls were busily responding to the UK invasion by manufacturing TV Beatles of their very own ("We're just trying to be friendly/ Come and watch us singing and play/We're the young generation/We got something to say", etc) a new awareness and lust for exploration (egged on, in part, by Sandoz) was creeping into the mystic. Psychedelic sounds beckoned, calling, in the words of the legendary Sky Saxon: "Upside down and turning around and wearing her funny frown – with one sinister glance the horse then stopped his prance . . . But slide out the lid of the music box and step into our green fields of giant flowers, plants and colored mist and escape for a while." Whatever that was supposed to mean . . .

57

The Lovin' Spoonful
'Daydream'

Label: **Pye International/Kama Sutra**
Date: **1966**

Includes: **Daydream • You Didn't Have To Be So Nice • Jug Band Music • Let The Boy Rock And Roll • Bald Headed Lena**

❞The second Lovin' Spoonful album (*Do You Believe In Magic?* being the first) is the complete mixture of folk, jug band and blues that the title track hit single merely hinted at. John Sebastian's songwriting is mature – there's a wealth of fine material in 'You Didn't Have To Be So Nice', 'Didn't Want To Have To Do It', 'Jug Band Music' – and riddled with wit and humour. 'Daydream' remains the most complete piece of Greenwich Village electric folk and has never been matched.❞ – B.H.

Musicians: **John Sebastian** (vocals, guitar) • **Zal Yanovsky** (vocals, guitar) • **Steve Boone** (bass) • **Joe Butler** (drums)

57a

The Lovin' Spoonful
'The Very Best Of The Lovin' Spoonful'

Label: **Kama Sutra/Kama Sutra**

Date: **1970**

Includes: **Do You Believe In Magic? • Summer In The City • Rain On The Roof • Six O'Clock • Darling Be Home Soon • Younger Girl**

❞For 'Summer In The City', the best song ever written about summer in the city, and 'Rain On The Roof', the best song ever written about gutter systems.❞ – **Ed.**

Musicians: As **Daydream**

58

The Mamas And The Papas
'If You Can Believe Your Eyes And Ears'

Label: **RCA/Dunhill**
Date: **1966**

Includes: **Straight Shooter • Go Where You Wanna Go • Spanish Harlem • The In Crowd • You Baby**

❞The experience of gigs in folk clubs and coffee-houses simply bursts from this album, a collection of completed and well-informed ideas. There's 'California Dreaming' and 'Monday Monday', naturally, amongst songs just as carefully written and conceived. The harmonies are perfect, the four voices blending and weaving throughout songs like 'Straight Shooter', 'Go Where You Wanna Go', 'Got A Feeling' and more, sounding totally natural and effortless. Eventually the group would become a virtual self-parody but here they are simply fascinating.❞ – B.H.

Musicians: **John Phillips • Michelle Phillips • Cass Elliott • Denny Doherty**

58a

The Mamas & The Papas
'Hits Of Gold'

Label: **Stateside/Dunhill**
Date: **1968**

Includes: **California Dreamin' • Dedicated To**

The One I Love • Monday Monday • You Baby • I Saw Her Again Last Night • Creeque Alley

❬❬ Endless summer until it turned chilly. **❭❭** – P.P.

Musicians: As **If You Can Believe Your Eyes And Ears**

59

The Turtles

'Happy Together Again – The Turtles Greatest Hits'

Label: **Philips/Sire**
Date: **1979**
(UK version is a single album/US is a double)

Includes: **Happy Together • You Showed Me • Me About You • Outside Chance • She'd Rather Be With Me • Elenore • Grim Reaper Of Love**

❬❬ The history of Californian sixties pop summed up in a single group. The Turtles followed the shifting trends – surf, folk-rock, protest, pseudo-psychedelia – with a cheeky opportunism, and, on occasions such as 'Outside Chance', 'Sound Asleep', 'Happy Together' (*the* summer smash of '67) and others, produced models that outshone the originals. Ginchy. **❭❭** – Ed.

Musicians: **Mark Volman** (vocals) • **Howard Kaylan** (vocals) • **Al Nichol** (guitar) • **Jim Tucker** (guitar) • **Don Murray** (drums) • **John Barbata** (drums) • **Jim Pons** (bass) • **John Seiter** (drums)

60

The Beach Boys

'Pet Sounds'

Label: **Capitol/Capitol**
Date: **1966**

Includes: **Wouldn't It Be Nice • God Only Knows • I Know There's An Answer • I Just Wasn't Made For These Times • Caroline No**

❬❬ The complete record – in many ways the first album as opposed to collection of tracks – a perfect creation. Here Brian Wilson fuses his own music which has been carefully developed through surf music, harmonies and fifties teen romanticism. The surf element, however, is missing and the other constituents are joined by a studio mastery which equals that of Phil Spector. The songs are unforgettable, classics of any era, and confirm *Pet Sounds* as a landmark in pop – and possibly its best ever album. **❭❭** – B.H.

Musicians: **Brian Wilson • Dennis Wilson • Carl Wilson • Mike Love • Al Jardine**

61

The Byrds

'Mr Tambourine Man'

Label: **CBS/Columbia**
Date: **1965**

Includes: **Mr Tambourine Man** • **I'll Feel A Whole Lot Better** • **The Bells Of Rhymney** • **All I Really Wanna Do** • **I Knew I'd Want You** • **Chimes Of Freedom**

ffNaturally following on the group's hit single, 'Mr Tambourine Man', this album forges a fascinating cross between folk music and bedat. Mixing some Dylan ('All I Really Want To Do', 'Spanish Harlem Incident') with interpretations of British traditional folk ('The Bells Of Rhymney') and startling originals such as Gene Clark's 'Feel A Whole Lot Better', its a record of jangling freshness where the moulding of two seemingly conflicting forms merges into something totally individuals. **JJ** – **B.H.**

Musicians: **Jim (Roger) McGuinn** (vocals, guitar) • **Gene Clark** (vocals) • **David Crosby** (vocals, guitar) • **Chris Hillman** (vocals, bass) • **Michael Clarke** (drums)

The Byrds

'Turn! Turn! Turn!'

Label: **CBS/Columbia**
Date: **1966**

Includes: **Turn! Turn! Turn/Set You Free This Time/Lay Down Your Weary Tune/The World Turns All Around Her/The Times They Are A-Changin'/Wait And See**

ffOn which the group refine the jangling folk-rock sound and make it their own, with graceful, compact harmonies and McGuinn's twelve-string splashing with merit. **JJ** – **Ed.**

Musicians: As **Mr Tambourine Man**

62

Bob Dylan

'Highway 61 Revisited'

Label: **CBS/Columbia**
Date: **1965**

Includes: **Like A Rolling Stone** • **It Takes A Lot To Laugh, It Takes A Train To Cry** • **From A Buick 6** • **Desolation Row** • **Highway 61 Revisited** • **Just Like Tom Thumb's Blues**

ffDylan's electric, and electrifying odyssey. The single most important voice in popular music, Dylan kicked pop into the twentieth century. *Highway 61* harnesses the street poetry of 'Like A Rolling Stone' to electric rhythms. From the sleeve notes to the audacious eleven minutes of 'Desolation Row', it's a perfect album. **JJ** – **P.H.**

ffStunning, diamond-hard performances of his greatest songs, howling in the face of derision . . . **JJ** – **A.S.**

ff'Like A Rolling Stone' is still Dylan's best song. **JJ** – **C.C.**

62a

Bob Dylan

'Bringing It All Back Home'

Label: **CBS/Columbia**
Date: **1965**

Includes: **Maggie's Farm** • **Subterranean Homesick Blues** • **Outlaw Blues** • **It's Alright Ma (I'm Only Bleeding)** • **Gates Of Eden**

ffBetween the folky drifter and the born again Christian who talks to animals, came the cynical, acerbic spitter whose malevolent wit prompted the folk purists to cry 'Judas!'. The response? – 'I don't believe you. You're a liar.' **JJ** – **Ed.**

ffDylan's first transition with an electric and an acoustic side. The latter continues the imagery of previous work, with the specific becoming more illusive, whereas the electric side is rough and harsh, freely bursting out of previous preconceptions. Dylan seems excited by the changes he is making, mischievous even, and the contrasts between the styles give the album its edge and unique atmosphere. **JJ** – B.H.

63

Paul Revere And The Raiders

'Midnight Ride'

Label: **CBS/Columbia**
Date: **1966**

Includes: **Hungry** • **Kicks** • **I'm Not Your Stepping Stone** • **Louie, Go Home** • **There She Goes** • **Ballad Of A Useless Man**

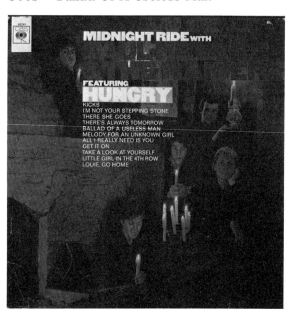

JJThe Raiders were, with little doubt, the most consistently good American mainstream pop band of the mid-sixties. They meant not a jot in Britain but in their homeland they became teen idols (and were thus derided by hipsters) through regular appearances on 'Where The Action Is' and a series of wonderfully-crafted commercial hits. Despite their weeny-appeal, however, there was nothing innocuous about the Raiders' music; just listen to the power and drive of 'I'm Not Your Stepping Stone' or 'Louie, Go Home' (which was desecrated by David Bowie on the B-side of his first single,

'Liza Jane', by the by). The Raiders spell at the top came to a close when certain persons plundered their musical style something rotten and fenced it to the Monkees. **JJ** – **Ed.**

JJProper American pop. **JJ** – **G.D.**

Musicians: **Mark Lindsay** (vocals, sax) • **Paul Revere** (keyboards) • **Philip Volk** (bass) • **Drake Levin** (guitar) • **Michael 'Smitty' Smith** (drums)

64

The Monkees

'Headquarters'

Label: **Colgems/RCA**
Date: **1967**

Includes: **You Told Me** • **Forget That Girl** • **You Just May Be The One** • **Shades Of Grey** • **Sunny Girlfriend** • **Zilch** • **No Time**

JJThe most perfect example of the brilliance that results from uninhibited love of the music. **JJ** – **M.M.**

Musicians: **Mike Nesmith** • **Micky Dolenz** • **Peter Tork** • **Davy Jones**

64a

The Monkees

'The Birds, The Bees & The Monkees'

Label: **RCA/Colgens**
Date: **1968**

Includes: **Dream World** • **Auntie's Municipal Court** • **Tapioca Tundra** • **Daydream Believer** • **PO Box 9847** • **Valleri** • **Zor & Zam**

JJTriumph through adversity. And proof that irritating advertising campaigns sometimes obscure worthy products. All the hippies who sneered at the Monkees were missing out on the fun. So they didn't play their instruments? Better to get someone to do it for you than to play mind-numbing extended oriental freak-out patterns into the night, I would have thought. But I digress from the fact that *The Birds, The Bees . . . ,* the Monkees fourth, was an album as worthy of attention as anything the majority of the hippie bands of the time were up to. Apart from the inclusion of the usual horrendous Davy Jones twee-tune ('We Were Made For Each Other'), every one's a winner. There's Mike Nesmith's left-field country vision ('Auntie's Municiapl Court', 'Tapioca Tundra'), there's broody experiment ('Writing Wrongs'), there's one of the most inspirational singles of all time ('Valleri'), there's Micky Dolenz's gripping Grace Slick imitation on the dramatic 'Zor & Zam', and bags more. So there. **))** – **Ed.**

Musicians: As **Headquarters**

something that was, for five minutes at least, unique. Ron Elliott remains one of the most ridiculously neglected pop creators of this twentieth century. **))** – **Ed.**

Musicians: **Ron Elliott** (guitar) ● **Sal Valentino** (vocals, guitar) ● **Ron Meagher** (bass) ● **Jon Peterson** (drums)

66

The Knickerbockers

'Lies' (UK title: 'The Fabulous Knickerbockers')

Label: **London/Challenge**
Date: **1966**

Includes: **Lies/I Can Do It Better/Can't You See I'm Trying/Just One Girl/I Believe In Her/Wishful Thinking**

((Of all the billions of bands that emerged in the States in the mid-sixties imitating the Fab Four, the Knickerbockers got closest to capturing the sound. In fact, they went a step beyond for, although their songs were merely carefully crafted copies of the Lennon-McCartney style, the energy and imagination they put into their delivery was beefier than anything the Beatles could manage on their first couple of albums. With a few more songs as twisterrific as 'Just One Girl', the Knickerbockers might have been able to escape the mop top shadow (and hence refrain from

65

The Beau Brummels

'The Original Hits Of The Beau Brummels'

Label: –/**JAS**
Date: **1975**

Includes: **Laugh Laugh** ● **Just A Little** ● **I Want You** ● **Don't Talk To Strangers** ● **In Good Time** ● **Sad Little Girl**

((Formed in San Francisco in 1964, the Beau Brummels provide the missing link (or one of them) between British Beat and the folk-rock sounds of the Byrds et al. The copped their style from the twelve-string jangle of the Searchers and yet, by leaving out the weedy R&B overtones of the Liverpudlians, produced

printing grovelling apologia such as 'You can't compare any other group to the Knicks because they are incomparable' on the back of their LP sleeves). **))** – **Ed.**

Musicians: **Buddy Randell** (sax) • **John Charles** (bass) • **Beau Charles** (guitar) • **Jimmy Walker** (drums)

67

Simon and Garfunkel

'Parsley, Sage, Rosemary and Thyme'

Label: **CBS/CBS**
Date: **1966**

Includes: **Scarborough Fair/Canticle** • **59th Street Bridge Song** • **The Dangling Conversation** • **A Simple, Desultory Philippic** • **For Emily, Whenever I May Find Her** • **7 O'Clock News/Silent Night**

((The dynamic duo's fey charm, their mannered college-boy wistfulness and infuriatingly perfect productions can't obscure the majesty of Paul Simon's songs or the fact that at least one (probably more) generation is going to go through life haunted by them. In fact, S delivered his grittiest, most ingeneous music without G, but *Parsley, Sage . . .* is probably their most rounded album, a blend of abrasiveness and sugar, painful observation and beauty. **))** – **E.W.**

Musicians: **Paul Simon** (guitar, vocals) • **Art Garfunkel** (vocals)

68

The Sonics

'Original Northwest Punk'

Label: **–/First American**
Date: **1977**

Includes: **The Witch** • **You've Got Your Head On Backwards** • **I'm A Man** • **Psycho** • **High Time** • **Maintaining My Cool**

((Inspired by the British R&B bands of the mid-Sixties, the Sonics from Washington State, USA, started doing it themselves in 1964. Or rather a *version* of it. More ravaged, raw, manky, sleazy, rough, dirty and stinky rock-beat music than this has never existed. Imagine, if you will, speaking to a friend 1,000 miles away on the telephone. In the apartment above your friend's, a rock group are playing extremely fast R&B extremely loudly through speakers that have been slashed to add that extra horror-fuzz tone. The singer's microphone appears to be blocked with some foreign matter – he is having to strain perilously and is blabbering incoherent non sequiturs in a monstrously nasal fashion. Suddenly your friend drops dead and you are left with nothing but that noise . . . and it is growing louder. That's the Sonics. And here are their most abrasive moments. **))** – **Ed.**

Musicians: **Andy Parypa** (bass) • **Gerry Roslie** (keyboards, vocals) • **Rob Lind** (sax, vocals) • **Larry Parypa** (guitar) • **Bob Bennett** (drums)

Blues Magoos

'Electric Comic Book'

Label: –/**Mercury**
Date: **1967**

Includes: **Pipe Dream • There's A Chance We Can Make It • Gloria • Albert Common Is Dead • Baby, I Want You • Rush Hour**

ʃʃFor once, Sixties' sleeve notes contained a hint of accuracy: '. . . the shotgun marriage of Pop Art and Looney Tunes . . .' On their second LP, New York's Blues Magoos abandon the psychedelic excesses of the first *Psychedelic Lollipop* to create a convincingly ravaged blend of power-pop and controlled acid rock. This album contains not only the most hysterical version of 'Gloria' ever committed to wax but a comic book insert which offers fans such commodities as a 'Psyche-De-Lite' which is 'a secret formula psychedelic lite that creates the wildest, wierdest shapes imaginable! It moves . . . it undulates . . . it'll blow your mind! The glowing red LAVA lives . . . breathes . . . fascinates! Wild! Only $9.95!' Get the picture? Ah, me, those were the days. **ʃʃ** – **Ed.**

Musicians: **Ralph Scala** (vocals, keyboards) • **Peppy Thielheim** (guitar, vocals) • **Ron Gilbert** (bass) • **Mike Exposito** (guitar) • **Geoff Daking** (drums)

The Standells

'Try It'

Label: –/**Tower**
Date: **1967**

Includes: **Trip To Paradise • Try It • Barracuda • Did You Ever Have That Feeling • All Fall Down • Riot On Sunset Strip**

ʃʃWith their final album, one of America's principal mid-sixties punk-beat bands provide the perfect summation of the era. Punky soul ('Ninety-Nine And A Half'), goes on pure-punk ('Barracuda') goes on folk-punk ('Poor Shell Of A Man') goes on punkedelia with inspirational backwards guitars ('All Fall Down') – all performed with maximum conviction and without glaring stylistic shifts. This band had something lacking in so many of their more celebrated and moneyed contemporaries – guileless, unaffected verve and super-sneers. This has been in my permanent Top Ten so long it'd take a court order to get it out. **ʃʃ** – **Ed.**

Musicians: **Larry Tamblyn** (vocals) • **Tony Valentino** (guitar) • **Dick Dodd** (drums) • **Gary Lane** (bass)

The Seeds

'Raw & Alive/The Seeds In Concert'

Label: **GNP Crescendo**/–
Date: **1968**

Includes: **Mr Farmer • No Escape • Up In Her Room • Gypsy Plays His Drums • 900 Million People Daily All Making Love • Pushin' Too Hard**

ʃʃTwo-chord punk meets the march of the flower children head on. In 1965 the legendary Sky Saxon achieved the impossible by writing a song even *simpler* than 'Louie Louie'. This, 'Pushin' Too Hard', went on to become a national hit and turn Saxon's band, the Seeds, into Los Angeles punk-beat heroes. The rest of the band's material was equally raw and simplistic and remained so until the end. For when the acid age dawned, the Seeds, instead of being abandoned by their audience, were hailed as flower-power lords despite the fact that they had made no stylistic shifts. This strange fact is possibly explained by Sky Saxon's eccentric blatherings which are heard to great effect on this LP. Over the doom-laden drone of the band, Sky mumbles and gibbers about 'forests outside your door', turning in a masterful performance and providing the perfect antidote to the Doors. 'This is the last song we have time to do. We'd like to dedicate it to society and the world because it still has a message,' drawls Sky before launching into the two-chord trash of 'Pushin' Too Hard'. And the message is: there is no message.)) – **Ed.**

Musicians: **Sky Saxon (Richard Marsh)** (vocals) • **Jan Savage** (bass) • **Rick Andridge** (drums) • **Daryl Hooper** (keyboards)

72

The Electric Prunes

'The Electric Prunes'

Label: **Reprise/Reprise**
Date: **1967**

Includes: **I Had Too Much To Dream (Last Night)** • **Bangles** • **Are You Lovin' Me More (But Enjoying It Less)** • **Get Me To The World On Time** • **Luvin'** • **Tunerville Trolley**

((West Coast art school punks whose influence on Jimi Hendrix and Todd Rundgren, to name but two, has never been acknowledged (largely because of their silly name). The

Prunes' sense of dynamics and mastery of technological effects (which are never used for their own sake) are awesome. This debut album contains two of the group's three indisputably classic moments – 'I Had Too Much To Dream' and 'Get Me To The World'. The third came on the subsequent LP *Underground* with 'The Great Banana Hoax' a song which undermines the Beatles *Sergeant Pepper* by misquoting from 'A Day In The Life' – 'I'd love to put you 0-0-0-0-0-0-0n' – and by having absolutely nothing to do with bananas (that's why it's a hoax, silly!).)) – **Ed.**

Musicians: **Jim Lowe** (vocals, guitar, autoharp) • **Weasel** (vocals, guitar) • **Ken Williams** (guitar) • **Mark Tulin** (bass, keyboards) • **Preston Ritter** (drums)

72a

The Electric Prunes

'Underground'

Label: **Reprise/Reprise**
Date: **1967**

Includes: **The Great Banana Hoax** • **Wind-Up Toys** • **Antique Doll** • **Dr Do-Good** • **I** • **Long Day's Flight**

((The sleeve notes have this to say: 'Black light/Flashing thoughts/Distinctiveness/Aggressiveness/Explosiveness/Possessiveness/Colored lights/Five multi-faceted/Weirdly connected/Ten Legs/Twelve arms/

One eye/One mind/One direction/Prunes, pits, stems/Shocking, electric!' I couldn't put it better myself. **JJ** – **Ed.**

Musicians: As **The Electric Prunes**

(Roger) Erickson (vocals, guitar) ● **Danny Thomas** (drums) ● **Dan Galindo** (bass)

73

The 13th Floor Elevators

'Easter Everywhere'

Label: – /International Artists
Date: **1979**

Includes: **Slip Inside This House** ● **She Lives (In A Time Of Her Own)** ● **Nobody To Love** ● **Earthquake** ● **Levitation** ● **Postures (Leave Your Body Behind)**

JJThe first psychedelic band – or so they claimed. Whether the claim is justified really doesn't matter for there was never anyone remotely like them anyway so why quarrel? The Elevators' music was a blend of R&B, Texas, cosmic delusions and too much acid. Their sound was the incessant bottle of Tommy Hall, bubbling over the reverberating guitar and desperate edge of Roky Erickson's voice. Their songs, originally harsh and simplistic, became beautiful and complex. Listen to 'She Lives' and see God. Listen to The 13th Floor Elevators and understand why they all went mad. (Too much, too soon.)**JJ** – **Ed.**

Musicians: **Tommy Hall** (vocals, bottle) ● **Roky**

74

The Byrds

'Fifth Dimension'

Label: **CBS/Columbia**
Date: **1966**

Includes: **5D** ● **Wild Mountain Thyme** ● **Eight Miles High** ● **I Come And Stand At Every Foor** ● **Hey Joe** ● **Captain Soul**

JJIf I were allowed but one record in my perfect collection, this would (I think) be it. The awesome, chilling atmosphere conjured by 'Eight Miles High' has yet to be equalled by man or beast, 'Hey Joe' has yet to be executed with more bravado, the unrelenting depression of 'I Come And Stand At Every Door' has yet to be rivalled, etc. Go ride the Lear Jet baby. **JJ** – **Ed.**

JJMcGuinn's finest moments – 'Eight Miles High', 'I See You', 'Wild Mountain Thyme', '5D – a gem Ask Tom Verlaine, ask Robyn Hitchcock, ask Alex Chilton (ask Tom Hibbert)! McGuinn defines the concept of atonal guitar playing throughout this masterful record. **JJ** – **N.C.**

Musicians: **Roger McGuinn (vocals, guitar)** ● **David Crosby (vocals, guitar)** ● **Chris Hillman** (vocals, bass) ● **Michael Clarke** (drums)

It's a near perfect collection – still within the Byrds' pop mainstream yet still displaying strong progression. **JJ** – **B.H.**

Musicians: As **Fifth Dimension**

74a

The Byrds

'Younger Than Yesterday'

Label: **CBS/Columbia**
Date: **1967**

Includes: **So You Wanna Be A Rock And Roll Star** ● **CTA 102** ● **Time Between** ● **Have You Seen Her Face** ● **My Back Pages** ● **Why**

ffAn important and intriguing album that contains the first forages into the realms of country rock – witness the unsurpassable guitar solo of the late Clarence White on Hillman's 'Time Between'. 'So You Wanna Be A Rock And Roll Star', on the other hand, is dizzy, electrified pop/rock music of the highest calibre. If it were not for the dreadful excesses of David Crosby's 'Mind Gardens', a song of monstrous conceit that quotes from Shakespeare in most pompous fashion, *Younger Than Yesterday* might replace *Fifth Dimension* as the Byrds finest hour (or forty minutes to be more accurate). **JJ** – **Ed.**

ffOn *Younger Than Yesterday*, the individuality of each group member peaks, yet still allows a complete group sound. There's the David Crosby of 'Renaissance Fair' and 'Everybody's Been Burned', the Chris Hillman of 'Thoughts And Words' and 'Have You Seen Her Face', while Roger McGuinn is the overseer, his influence implicit rather than explicit.

Late-Sixties/UK

Though Britain, too, embraced flower-power and the psychedelic spectre for half a fleeting moment, few apart from Syd Barrett could get it right. Acid flirtations were soon put aside by the vital musical query: 'Can the White Men play the Blues?' The deification of Eric Clapton was to lead to the age of the guitar hero as technical ability/virtuosity superceded passion/charisma in importance. Clapton is faster than Page is faster than Beck is faster than Lee is faster than Hendrix, argued the boys, tossing their long greasy hair as their 'chicks' sat in the corner sewing patches on filthy jeans and widening loon pants. The hippie girls took English folk-rock to their hearts and some of the boys went there too. But for most, 'progressive' rock was the thing. 'Progressive'? Where on earth, pray, was it going? . . .

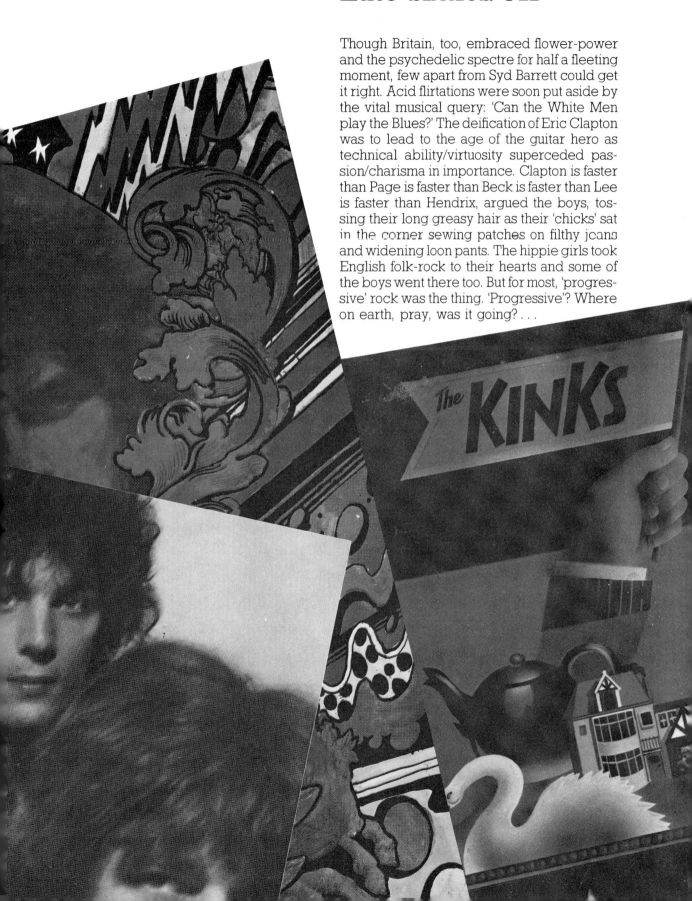

The Beatles

'Hey Jude'

Label: –/Capitol
Date: 1970

Includes: **Paperback Writer • Rain • Revolution • Old Brown Shoe • Don't Let Me Down • Ballad Of John And Yoko**

❝As much a mid-Sixties artefact as a late one – but where else to place it? This is a strange but wizard compilation and the only Beatles LP I can play all the way through without skipping. All the official albums have moments of cringing awfulness ('Michelle' on *Rubber Soul*, 'Yellow Submarine' on *Revolver*, 'She's Leaving Home' and 'When I'm 64' on *Sergeant Pepper*, 'Maxwell' and 'Octupus' on *Abbey Road*, etc) but this has no shaky moments. Only 'Rain', the best song Lennon ever wrote and the best the Beatles ever recorded.❞ – **Ed.**

Musicians: **Not Charles Hawtrey and the Deaf-Aids**

76

The Beatles

'The Beatles' (The White Album)

Label: **Apple/Apple**
Date: **1968 (double)**

Includes: **Back In The USSR • Glass Onion • While My Guitar Gently Weeps • Happiness Is A Warm Gun • Piggies • Julia • Birthday • Sexy Sadie • Revolution 1 • Revolution 9 • Everybody's Got Something To Hide Except Me And My Monkey**

❝An album of precious moments flirts with being disjointed but emerges as a true collection from a changing group.❞ – **B.K.**

❝Because.❞ – **M.W.**

❝Provides the vital missing link 'twixt the Marmalade and Charlie Manson.❞ – **Ed.**

Musicians: **Eric Clapton**

77

The Rolling Stones

'Beggars Banquet'

Label: **Decca/London**
Date: **1968**

Includes: **Sympathy For The Devil • No Expectations • Parachute Woman • Street Fighting Man • Stray Cat Blues • Factory Girl**

❝Opinions differ as to which is the best Stones album, but this IS it. Perfect from conception to resolution with no post-1970 compromises.❞ – **M.W.**

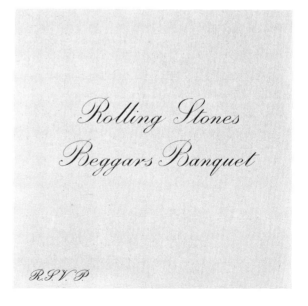

Musicians: **Mick Jagger** (vocals) • **Keith Richard** (guitar) • **Brian Jones** (guitar) • **Bill Wyman** (bass) • **Charlie Watts** (drums)

78

Pink Floyd

'Piper At The Gates Of Dawn'

Label: **Columbia/Tower**
Date: **1967**

Includes: **Astronomy Domine** • **Lucifer Sam** • **Pow R Toc H** • **Interstellar Overdrive** • **The Gnome** • **The Scarecrow**

❝Genuine innovation from Syd Barrett and a competent backing group. The originality of structure, and depth of space-guitar power as displayed on 'Astronomy Domine' baffles musical scientists to this day. Syd has gone and the Floyd continue to shamble about searching for that lost chord.❞ – Ed.

Musicians: **Syd Barrett** (guitar, vocals) • **Roger Waters** (guitar) • **Richard Wright** (keyboards) • **Nick Mason** (drums)

79

Syd Barrett

'The Madcap Laughs'/'Barrett' (Repackage of two albums)

Label: **Harvest/Harvest**

Date: 1974

Includes: **Terrapin** • **No Man's Land** • **Here I Go** • **Octopus** • **Long Gone** • **She Took A Long Cold Look** • **Baby Lemonade** • **Rats** • **Gigolo Aunt** • **Effervescing Elephant**

❝Because he really didn't care.❞ – G.D.

❝The man who launched 1,000 split knee loons shows the Floyd how it should be done before turning into a hamburger with a colour TV.❞ – C.P.L. and F.K.

80

John Mayall

'Bluesbreakers'

Label: **Decca/–**
Date: **1966**

Includes: **All Your Love** • **Hideaway** • **Steppin' Out** • **Ramblin' On My Mind** • **Parchman Farm**

❝By mid-1966, a vast army was being deployed – remnants of the very early Sixties R&B underground, disaffected mods, bespectacled sixth formers and camp followers were trying to grow sideburns, contemplating the greatcoat for winter wear and wondering whether smoking black might be cooler than taking French blues. Their hero was Eric Clapton whose reputation had been established, following his departure from the Yardbirds, by constant touring with Mayall, playing small halls, beat cellars and mod all-nighters, during which he perfected the technique that was to bring him superstardom with Cream. This LP was to become one of the essential components of any hip record collection of the era. It spurred the army to work chalking 'Clapton Is God' on brick walls throughout England and inspired battalions of imitators who would provide trained and skilful artisans for all future British bands through to the Clash.❞ – S.L.

(Editor's note: That's all very well but the unwary should be warned that this LP contains the worst drum solo in recorded history.)

Musicians: **John Mayall** (vocals, guitar, keyboards) • **Eric Clapton** (guitar) • **John McVie** (bass) • **Hughie Flint** (drums)

81

Cream

'Disraeli Gears'

Label: **Reaction/Atco**
Date: 1967

Includes: **Strange Brew** • **Sunshine Of Your Love** • **Dance The Night Away** • **Tales Of Brave Ulysses** • **Swlabr** • **We're Going Wrong**

ffBefore being gobbled up by a ghastly extended solo monster, Cream were mixing blues forms with vaguely psychedelic pop with varying degrees of success. This, their second album, is their most winning stab. **JJ** – **Ed.**

ffGreat cover. Music to climb amplifier towers by. **JJ** – **P.P.**

Musicians: **Jack Bruce** (vocals, bass) • **Eric Clapton** (guitar, vocals) • **Ginger Baker** (drums)

82

Jimi Hendrix

'Electric Ladyland'

Label: **Track/Reprise**
Date: 1968 (double)

Includes: **House Burning Down** • **All Along The Watchtower** • **And The Gods Made Love** • **Burning Of The Midnight Lamp** • **Voodoo Chile** • **1983 . . . (A Merman I Shall Be)**

ffThe only album Hendrix was happy with – which is good enough for me. A masterpiece. **JJ** – **H.S.**

Musicians: **Jimi Hendrix** (guitar, vocals) • **Noel Redding** (bass) • **Mitch Mitchell** (drums) • and others

83

Family

'Music In A Doll's House'

Label: **Reprise/Reprise**
Date: 1968

Includes: **The Chase** • **Old Songs New Songs** • **Hey Mr Policeman** • **See Through Windows** • **Peace Of Mind** • **The Breeze**

ffA mass of undisciplined, and seemingly unrelated, studio experiment and trickery make this debut album into something that (judging from the group's subsequent, orthodox and pedestrian efforts) it was never intended to be – a semi-classic of deranged invention. Phased violins, backward sax loops, lashings of feedback and Roger Chapman's uncommon voice taking care of the trippy imagery; all sounds quite spooky when one's examining the eerie cover simultaneously. **JJ** – **Ed.**

Musicians: **Roger Chapman** (vocals) • **Charlie Whitney** (guitar) • **Rick Grech** (bass) • **Jim King** (sax, woodwind) • **Rob Townsend** (drums)

84

Colosseum

'Those Who Are About To Die Salute You'

Label: **Fontana/–**
Date: 1968

Includes: **Walking In The Park** • **Mandarin** • **Debut** • **Beward The Ides Of March** • **Those About To Die**

ffTom Hibbert's favourite group.* Certainly one of Chris Welch's with the band reaching a pitch of instrumental hysteria unknown before or since. Cerebral metal goes flying. **JJ** – **C.W.**

*This is almost certainly a joke. – Ed.

Musicians: **Jon Hiseman** (drums) • **Dick Heckstall-Smith** (sax) • **Dave Greenslade** (keyboards) • **James Litherland** (guitar) • **Tony Reeves** (bass)

85

Spooky Tooth
'Spooky Two'

Label: **Island/A&M**
Date: **1969**

Includes: **Waiting For The Wind** • **Evil Woman** • **Feelin' Bad** • **Hangman Hang My Shell On A Tree**

((Strong, assured, 'no-nonsense' hard rock with tunes and the grinding organ of Gary Wright before he went deeply conceptual and platinum. The guitar solo of Luther Grosvenor on 'Evil Woman' is quite awesome and defies all phantoms.**))** – **Ed.**

Musicians: **Mike Harrison** (vocals) • **Gary Wright** (keyboards) • **Luther Grosvenor** (guitar) • **Mike Kellie** (drums) • **Greg Ridley** (bass)

86

Status Quo
'The Status Quo File'

Label: **Pye/–**
Date: **1977**

Includes: **Pictures Of Matchstick Men** • **Black Veils Of Melancholy** • **When My Mind Is Not Live** • **Ice In The Sun** • **Down The Dust Pipe** • **In My Chair** • **Mean Girl**

((BOOGIE!!! But let us not forget just what a superb flower-power pop band Quo were before they discovered twelve-bars and denim. 'When My Mind Is Not Live' is only one of the quasi-psychedelic mini-masterpieces an offer within this distinguished double compilation (of, mainly, late sixties stuff).**))** – **Ed.**

Musicians: **Francis Rossi** (guitar, vocals) • **Alan Lancaster** (bass) • **Rick Parfitt** (guitar, vocals) • **John Coghlan** (drums) • **Roy Lynes** (keyboards)

87

Love Sculpture
'Blues Helping'

Label: **Parlophone/Rare Earth**
Date: **1968**

Includes: **3 O'Clock Blues** • **I Believe To My Soul** • **On The Road Again** • **Wang-Dang-Doodle** • **Shake Your Hips** • **Blues Helping**

((Love Sculpture were the best of the late-sixties British 'blues boom' bands (admittedly a somewhat motley crew anyway) – possibly because, as later became evident, Dave Edmunds was one of the few guitarists who wasn't boringly purist and reverential about the form.**))** – **Ed.**

Musicians: **Dave Edmunds** (guitar, vocals, keyboards) • **John Williams** (bass) • **Bob 'Congo' Jones** (drums)

Jeff Beck

'Beck-Ola'

Label: **Columbia/Epic**
Date: 1969

Includes: **All Shook Up** • **Spanish Boots** • **Plynth (Water Down The Drain)** • **Hangman's Knee** • **Rice Pudding**

❪❪The definitive 'guitar hero' statement. The musical material is so subservient to what Beck's up to that it's almost irrelevant (as is the presence of singer Rod Stewart whose voice is, thankfully, plunged way down in the mix). While the rhythm section and Hopkins' piano plonk away, as if anyone is taking any notice of them, Beck shows off all his party tricks and, against one's better judgement, one has to be impressed.❫❫ – Ed.

Musicians: **Jeff Beck** (guitar) • **Nicky Hopkins** (piano) • **Ron Wood** (bass) • **Tony Newman** (drums) • **Rod Stewart** (vocals)

Led Zeppelin

Fourth album (no title)

Label: **Atlantic/Atlantic**
Date: 1971

Includes: **Black Dog** • **The Battle Of Evermore**

• **Stairway To Heaven** • **Misty Mountain Hop**

❪❪It's got 'Stairway To Heaven' on it. What more need one say?❫❫ – H.S.

Musicians: **Jimmy Page** (guitar) • **Robert Plant** (vocals) • **John Paul Jones** (bass) • **John Bonham** (drums)

Procol Harum

'A Salty Dog'

Label: **Regal Zonophone/A&M**
Date: 1969

Includes: **A Salty Dog** • **The Devil Came From Kansas** • **Pilgrim's Progress** • **The Milk Of Human Kindness**

❪❪The Orson Welles of rock music. Procol will always be remembered for 'A Whiter Shade Of Pale' but this, their third album, is their finest hour. An epic, sweeping achievement. The ideal mixture of rock rhythms to classical influences. The best example of that frequently attempted blend, Procol Harum pulled it off.❫❫ – P.H.

Musicians: **Gary Brooker** (vocals, keyboards) • **Matthew Fisher** (vocals, keyboards) • **Robin Trower** (guitar) • **Dave Knights** (bass) • **B. J. Wilson** (drums)

The Kinks

'Arthur Or The Decline And Fall Of The British Empire'

Label: **Pye/Reprise**
Date: 1969

Includes: **Victoria** • **Some Mother's Son** • **Australia** • **Mr Churchill Says** • **Young And Innocent Days** • **Drivin'**

❪❪The Kinks' second 'concept' album ([*The Kinks Are*] *The Village Green Preservation Society* was the first) sees Ray Davies looking back at twentieth century Britain with mingling affection and bitterness. Extraordinary songs (of course) pivot around 'Mr Churchill Says' which turns the Second World War into a disturbing raga-rock movement. The Empire totters and everybody gets deeply depressed in suburbia, wallowing in nostalgia and polishing the car that never goes anywhere. **JJ** – **Ed.**

Musicians: **Ray Davies** (vocals, guitar) ● **Dave Davies** (guitar) ● **John Dalton** (bass) ● **Mick Avory** (drums)

92

The Incredible String Band

'The 5000 Spirits Or The Layers Of The Onion'

Label: Elektra/Elektra
Date: 1967

Includes: **Chinese White** ● **Painting Box** ● **Little Cloud** ● **The Eyes Of Fate** ● **The Hedgehog's Song** ● **Way Back In The 1960's**

ffRidiculous Celtic hippies who were uniquely mad!**JJ** – **I.B.**

Musicians: **Robin Williamson** ● **Mike Heron** ● and others

93

Fairport Convention

'Liege And Lief'

Label: Island/A&M
Date: 1969

Includes: **Matty Groves** ● **Farewell, Farewell** ● **The Deserter** ● **Tam Lin** ● **Crazy Man Michael**

ffBritish folk-rock's finest hour. Fairport weren't the first people to realise the possibilities of fusing traditional folk music to electric rock rhythms – they just did it best. The album showcases the group's instrumental dexterity with an innate understanding of their traditional sources. An audacious experiment that paid off. **JJ** – **P.H.**

Musicians: **Sandy Denny** (vocals) ● **Simon Nicol** (vocals, guitar) ● **Richard Thompson** (guitar) ● **Ashley Hutchings** (bass) ● **Dave Swarbrick** (violin) ● (**Dave Mattacks** (drums)

Late-Sixties/US

Turn on, tune in, drop out. All across the nation there was a new vibration of love, peace and LSD. Free the people and kill the pigs. But for all the wonky naïvety of the new youth ideology, the spokesmen did manage to produce some exhilarating music for a while at least. In San Francisco the Dead and the Airplane did their 'thing', whilst down in L.A., Spirit and Love did a better one. And while most were busy 'expressing themselves' through extended acid freak-out symphonies, a few laid down the roots of rural country-rock. Meanwhile, on the other side of the continent, a healthy street-punk cynicism reared its ugly head in the form of Velvet Fugs and Godz. Somewhere in the middle a tiny voice spoke up for the bubblegum chewing kiddies saying; "Yummy yummy yummy/I've got love in my tummy." Strange days, indeed. The past is a foreign country – they do things differently there . . .

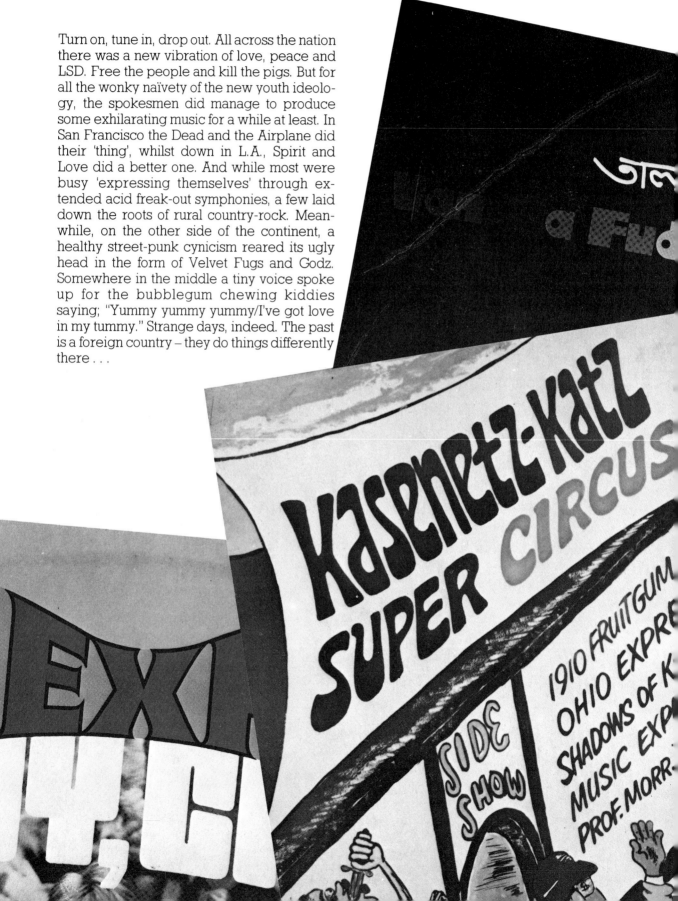

The Turtles

'Turtle Soup'

Label: – /White Whale
Date: 1969

Includes: **House On The Hill** • **She Always Leaves Me Laughing** • **Love In The City** • **John & Julie** • **Hot Little Hands** • **Somewhere Friday Nite**

One of the five very best albums of the Sixties in the estimation of this listener. Sensing that their moments of pop stardom were up, the Turtles entered the studio to record one last long player under the production auspices of Kink Ray Davies. How much control the old soak from Muswell Hill actually took over the record is uncertain, but its raw, low-key production exhibited the band's strength of performance as never before. Less kooky and ebullient, more subdued than the Turtles' previous work, this was the first time they had used nothing but original material on album. And one can only wonder why they waited so long, piddling about with mediocre Bonner/ Gordon and P. F. Sloan work and dodgy Nilsson numbers. These songs are magic bits of low-key love/cerebral celebration, from 'Love In The City' a beautiful ballad that builds to a binding hook, to 'Hot Little Hands', a manic squeaker that sounds like the Velvet Underground on something not very nice; from 'She Always Leaves Me Laughing', a charge of feigned joy, to 'Somewhere Friday Night' which is a regular tear-jerker and no mistake. This is the stuff pop legends are supposed to be made of but due to circumstances not a million miles away from a near-zero sales situation, 'Turtle Soup' proved to be just a silent bye-bye. Artistically, however, a fitting end to the story of Californian pop. – **Ed.**

Musicians: **Mark Volman** (vocals) • **Howard Kaylan** (vocals) • **Al Nichol** (guitar, keyboards) • **Jim Pons** (bass) • **John Seiter** (drums)

Moby Grape

'Moby Grape'

Label: **CBS/Columbia**
Date: 1967

Includes: **Hey Grandma** • **Mr Blues** • **8.05** • **Omaha** • **Ain't No Use** • **Indifference**

Moby Grape were in the wrong place at the wrong time. Of all the late Sixties San Francisco bands, they were the most creative and imaginative but their catchy power-pop/blues and country-tinged balladry was completely out of step with the psychedelic improvisatory style of their contemporaries. The Grape cause was further hindered by the over-the-top publicity heaped upon this debut album (five singles drawn from the LP and released simultaneously, bottles of 'Moby Grape' juice given away at concerts, etc.) at a time when commercial 'Hype' tendencies were becoming increasingly unfashionable. In another era, Moby Grape might have developed into a truly commercial force for, in Peter Lewis, Bob Moseley and the eccentric Skip Spence, they boasted a triumvirate of talented, individual yet complimentary songwriters who here present their work to best advantage. **JJ** – **Ed.**

JJA perfect debut album, *Moby Grape* lies somewhere between mid-Sixties pop and San Franciscan experiment with the group's many ideas crammed into short songs. There are strong four-part harmonies or a solo voice, soft country-rock or hard lead guitar, music simultaneously safe and challenging. Tight and confident with a unique breadth and power. **JJ** – **B.H.**

Musicians: **Skip Spence** (guitar, vocals) ● **Peter Lewis** (guitar, vocals) ● **Jerry Miller** (guitar, vocals) ● **Bob Mosley** (bass, vocals) ● **Don Stevenson** (drums)

96

Jefferson Airplane

'Surrealistic Pillow'

Label: **RCA/RCA**
Date: **1967**

Includes: **Somebody To Love** ● **White Rabbit** ● **Three-Fifths Of A Mile** ● **DCBA 25** ● **Plastic Fantastic Lover** ● **Coming Back To Me**

JJRecorded and released as flower-power was grabbing world-wide attention, *Surrealistic Pillow* was an obvious part of that fashion and musical environment, but restrained itself from the period's excesses. Instead, it proved to be a tangent of folk-rock and psychedelia, mutating into something else again. **JJ** – **B.H.**

JJThe soaring, quasi-masculine voice of Grace Slick is bolstered by the tones of Marty Balin and Paul Kantner to invest the group with a unique three part vocal attack – unique, at any rate, in terms of the hard, acidic rock served up by Jorma Kaukonen's naked guitar aggression and the devious fullness of Jack Casady's fluid bass guitar patterns. **JJ** – **K.K.**

Musicians: **Marty Balin** (vocals) ● **Grace Slick** (vocals) ● **Paul Kantner** (guitar, vocals) ● **Jorma Kaukonen** (guitar) ● **Jack Casady** (bass) ● **Spencer Dryden** (drums)

97

Grateful Dead

'Live Dead'

Label: **Warner Bros/Warner Bros**
Date: **1970 (double)**

Includes: **Dark Star** ● **St Stephen** ● **The Eleven** ● **Death Don't Have No Mercy**

JJThe Dead epitomised acid madness, something hard to contain or fake in a studio, but *live* . . . **JJ** – **M.W.**

Musicians: **Jerry Garcia** (vocals, guitar) ● **Bob Weir** (vocals, guitar) ● **Rod 'Pigpen' McKernan** (keyboards, vocals) ● **Phil Lesh** (bass) ● **Tom 'TC' Constanten** (keyboards) ● **Bill Kreutzmann** (drums) ● **Micky Hart** (drums)

98

Quicksilver Messenger Service

'Quicksilver Messenger Service'

Label: **Capitol/Capitol**
Date: **1968**

Includes: **Pride Of Man** ● **Dino's Song** ● **Gold And Silver** ● **Too Long** ● **The Fool**

JJCaptures the San Francisco acid era at its purest – before the dream faded. The group's second LP, *Happy Trails,* is generally regarded as their best but this debut is free of the latter's indulgences. Packed with sensitive vocals, fine guitar playing, interesting material, and more. **JJ** – **N.C.**

Musicians: **Gary Duncan** (vocals, guitar) ● **John Cipollina** (guitar) ● **David Freiberg** (bass, vocals) ● **Greg Elmore** (drums)

99

Country Joe And The Fish

'Electric Music For The Mind And Body'

Label: **Vanguard/Vanguard**
Date: **1967**

Includes: **Flying High** ● **Not So Sweet Martha Lorraine** ● **Death Sound** ● **Porpoise Mouth** ● **Superbird** ● **Grace**

❪❪Psychedelic jug band that offers political and topical overtones as well as chronicling accurately the atmosphere of the times (and the prevailing drug culture). Barry Melton's guitar work is nothing less than amazing and the songs balance the imagery of Country Joe McDonald's lyrics uncannily. Here is the essence of 1967 California. ❫❫ – **B.H.**

Musicians: **Country Joe McDonald** (vocals, guitar, harmonica) ● **Barry Melton** (guitar) ● **David Cohen** (keyboards) ● **Bruce Barthol** (bass) ● **Chicken Hirsh** (drums)

100

Spirit

'Spirit'

Label: **CBS/Ode-Epic**
Date: **1968**

Includes: **Fresh Garbage** ● **Uncle Jack** ● **Mechanical World** ● **Straight Arrow** ● **Gramophone Man** ● **The Great Canyon Fire In General**

❪❪A near perfect blend of acid rock, garage psychedelia and pure pop with a spattering of jazz crumbs thrown in for luck. Jay Ferguson's songs are immensely persuasive and the guitar antics of madcap Randy California are, for once, controlled. As so often in the kooky world of rock 'n' roll, first proves best. ❫❫ – **Ed.**

Musicians: **Mark Andes** (bass, vocals) ● **Cassidy** (drums, percussion) ● **Randy California** (guitar) ● **John Locke** (keyboards) ● **Jay Ferguson** (vocals, percussion)

100a

Spirit

'Twelve Dreams Of Dr Sardonicus'

Label: **Epic/Epic**
Date: **1970**

Includes: **Nature's Way** ● **Animal Zoo** ● **Mr Skin** ● **Space Child** ● **Street Worm** ● **Morning Will Come**

❪❪10,000 potatoes can't be wrong. ❫❫ – **P.C.**

Musicians: As **Spirit**

101

Love

'Da Capo'

Label: **Elektra/Elektra**
Date: **1967**

Includes: **7 And 7 Is** ● **She Comes In Colors** ● **The Castle** ● **Revelation**

❪❪Whilst most other critics go potty about *Forever Changes,* one at least finds Love's second album far more thrilling. It catches the group in mid-metamorphosis as they change from LA punksters to zonked-out flits before your very ears. The punky rush of the stimulating '7 And 7 Is' (complete with nuclear test noises), the baroque tendencies of 'The Castle', and the free-form mind excursions of the seventeen minute 'Revelation' are, I'm convinced, a major contribution to shifting West Coast styles. ❫❫ – **Ed.**

Musicians: **Arthur Lee** (guitar, vocals) ● **John Echols** (guitar) ● **Bryan MacLean** (guitar, vocals) • **Alban 'Snoopy' Pfisterer** (drums, percussion) • **Michael Stuart** (drums, percussion) • **Tjay Cantrelli** (percussion) • **Ken Forssi** (bass)

101a

Love

'Forever Changes'

Label: **Elektra/Elektra**
Date: **1967**

Includes: **Alone Again Or** • **Andmoreagain** • **The Daily Planet** • **The Red Telephone** • **Live And Let Live** • **Bummer In The Summer**

❝A remarkable collection of haunting, sometimes surrealistic songs, based on acoustic Spanish guitars and embellished with string sections and occasional brass. The arrangements are impeccable, understated but unhesitating, overrun by the voice of Arthur Lee (or occasionally Bryan MacLean). Poignant, accessible and timeless music.❞ – **B.H.**

❝A band whose remarkable innocations were destroyed by personal lack of discipline.❞ – **J.T.**

❝Considering this album is a contemporary of the Beatles' *Sergeant Pepper,* it's hardly surprising that the genius of Love and Arthur Lee was overshadowed. But it's a drag. No-one worth their salt can afford to be without an album that contains lyrics like: 'The snot has caked against my pants.'❞ – **C.P.L. & F.K.**

Musicians: As **Da Capo,** without Pfisterer and Cantrelli

102

The Doors

'The Doors'

Label: **Elektra/Elektra**
Date: **1967**

Includes: **Break On Through** • **The Crystal Ship** • **Light My Fire** • **Back Door Man** • **End Of The Night** • **The End**

❝The debut of one of the most exciting, charismatic and influential bands the world will ever see.❞ – **J.T.**

❝The encapsulation of Morrison's visions of the abyss and the power of sex.❞ – **H.S.**

Musicians: **Jim Morrison** (vocals) • **Ray Manzarek** (keyboards) • **Bobby Krieger** (guitar) • **John Densmore** (drums)

103

Captain Beefheart And His Magic Band

'Safe As Milk'

Label: **Pye/Buddah**
Date: **1967**

Includes: **Dropout Boogie** • **Electricity** • **Yellow Brick Road** • **Abba Zaba** • **Plastic Factory** • **Autumn's Child**

❝The missing link between Howlin' Wolf and whatever came next, if it ever did. A true originals, a shiny man who not only didn't give a damn but didn't give it with *honesty*.❞ – **Ed.**

❝Every record collection has to have at least one LP by a genius like Captain Beefheart – and I vote for this one. (P.S.: The artistic descent of guitarist Ry Cooder from *Safe As Milk* to the pits of *The Slide Area* as long and tragic.)❞ – **N.C.**

❝The first in a line of unique records from Don Van Vliet, *aka* Captain Beefheart. *Safe As Milk* is mostly blues-based, albeit in an original way, with Howlin' Wolf the most obvious influence. But in a line similar to the later British

R&B groups, the music is interpreted with total originality – thus the electricity of 'Electricity', the surreal stop of 'Abba Zaba' and the bizarre outgrowth on Robert Pete Williams' 'Grown So Ugly'. Beefheart's band really *is* magic: Jeff Cotton and Ry Cooder play exhilarating guitar passages and the whole album is powerful, exciting and progressive, laying foundations for the Captain's later music but also existing as superlatively unique in its own right. **JJ** – **B.H.**

ffThe 25th Century pilgrim crashes out of Death Valley in order to zing line your sanity with the secret of electricity – acid slide guitar courtesy of Ry Cooder who was never quite the same after he forsook the Magic Band for Yank Rachel. **JJ** – **C.P.L. & F.K.**

Musicians: **Captain Beefheart (Don Van Vliet)** (vocals) **Antennae Jim Semens (Jeff Cotton)** (guitar) ● **Ry Cooder** (guitar) ● **Drumbo (John French)** (drums) ● **Jerry Handley** (bass) ● **Snouffer (Alex St Claire)** (guitar)

104

The Byrds

'The Notorious Byrd Brothers'

Label: **CBS/Columbia**
Date: **1968**

Includes: **Goin' Back** ● **Draft Morning** ● **Wasn't Born To Follow** ● **Change Is Now** ● **Dolphins Smile** ● **Tribal Gathering**

ffAnother near-perfect album from the Byrds. Previous harsh edges are left behind in favour of a more harmonic whole. Country stuff and spacey bits gell together in a bed of further studio exploration to create another dimension. I'm making it appear 'mellow and laid-back' when in fact it's more sort of, er, atmospherically sweet and sour. A tricky one to describe. A grand feat. **JJ** – **Ed.**

Musicians: **Roger McGuinn** (vocals, guitar) ● **Chris Hillman** (vocals, bass) ● **Mike Clarke** (drums)

105

The Band

'Music From Big Pink'

Label: **Capitol/Capitol**
Date: **1968**

Includes: **Caledonia Mission** ● **Long Black Veil** ● **I Shall Be Released** ● **The Weight** ● **Chest Fever**

ffProfoundly influential – the whole of the American rural dream in one album. **JJ** – **H.S.**

Musicians: **Robbie Robertson** (guitar) ● **Rick Danko** (bass, vocals) ● **Levon Helm** (drums, mandolin, vocals) ● **Richard Manuel** (drums, keyboards, vocals) ● **Garth Hudson** (keyboards, sax)

106

Buffalo Springfield

'Again'

Label: **Atlantic/Atco**
Date: **1968**

Includes: **Mr Soul** ● **Expecting To Fly** ● **Bluebird** ● **Hung Upside Down** ● **Rock 'n' Roll Woman** ● **Broken Arrow**

ffThe birth of Neil Young. The savage HM pop of 'Mr Soul', the haunting 'Expecting To Fly' and the heartbeat college experiment of 'Broken Arrow' all point to a developing talent. His cohorts, Furay and Stills, despite the fact they were soon to become aggravating tootly-tootly steel-nose whiners, acquit themselves with dignity too. **JJ** – **Ed.**

Musicians: **Neil Young** (guitar, vocals) • **Stephen Stills** (guitar, vocals) • **Richie Furay** (guitar, vocals) • **Bruce Palmer** (bass) • **Dewey Martin** (drums) • and others

107

The Flying Burrito Bros
'The Gilded Palace Of Sin'

Label: **A&M/A&M**
Date: **1969**

Includes: **Christine's Tune** • **Sin City** • **Dark End Of The Street** • **Wheels** • **Do You Know How It Feels** • **Hippie Boy**

ʕʕHaving invented 'country-rock', with a little help from Chris Hillman and Roger McGuinn, on the Byrds' 1968 album *Sweetheart Of The Rodeo,* Gram Parsons left to form his own group (taking Hillman with him) and to define the genre further. This debut Burrito's album remains the best example of a form that would soon fall into disrepute at the hands of Poco, the Eagles and others. The thin, unrefined production, the understated chug, the crack in Parsons' voice and the garish 'Nudie' suits on the back cover are deeply fab, y'all. Only the self-conscious marijuana plants on G.P.'s jacket hint at irksome parody.ʔʔ – **Ed.**

Musicians: **Gram Parsons** (vocals, guitar) • **Chris Hillman** (guitar, bass) • **Chris Ethridge** (bass) • **Sneaky Pete Kleinow** (pedal steel guitar) • **Jon Corneal** (drums)

108

Sir Douglas Quintet
'Mendocino'

Label: **Mercury/Smash**
Date: **1969**

Includes: **She's About A Mover** • **Mendocino** • **I Don't Want** • **At The Crossroads** • **If You Really Want Me To I'll Go** • **It Didn't Even Bring Me Down**

ʕʕRocky roll with Tex-Mex beat and the bubbly-fudge organ of Augie Meyers taking the Sooty-sound into a new dimension. 'Sir Douglas Quintet is back. We'd like to thank all of our beautiful friends all over the country for all their beautiful vibrations. We lurve you.'ʔʔ – **Ed.**

Musicians: **Doug Sahm** (vocals, guitar) • **Augie Meyer** (keyboard) • **Harvey Regan** (bass) • **John Perez**(drums) • **Frank Morin** (horns)

109

Creedence Clearwater Revival
'Bayou Country'

Label: **Liberty/Fantasy**
Date: **1969**

Includes: **Born On The Bayou** • **Keep On Chooglin'** • **Bootleg** • **Proud Mary** • **Graveyard Train**

ʕʕOut on a commercial limb of their own, Creedence's swamp rock 'n' roll proved to be one of the pop success stories of the Sixties. And rightly so. The songs and immaculate guitar of John Fogerty defy convention and serve up a refreshing alternative to the mind sprawls of most contemporaries.ʔʔ – **Ed.**

Musicians: **John Fogerty** (guitar, vocals) • **Tom Fogerty** (guitar) • **Doug Clifford** (drums) • **Stu Cook** (bass)

110

Ohio Express
'Chewy Chewy'

Label: **Buddah/Buddah**
Date: **1968**

Includes: **Chewy Chewy** • **Nothing Sweeter Than My Baby** • **1, 2, 3, Red Light** • **Little Girl** • **Fun** • **Down In Tennessee**

ʕʕTowards the end of 1967, Jerry Kasenetz and Jeff Katz invented bubblegum music in order to free the world from the indulgent 'progressive' free-form acid-jam tendencies raining down all over. Sadly, this plan failed but they did make pots of mney and plenty of disposable pop. Nearly all the bubblegum classics of the era were written, or co-written, by the brilliant Joey Levine and 'Chewy Chewy' stands as the ultimate statement of his art. **))** – **Ed.**

((Their absolute classic! Brilliant enough to get your dentures clicking along. What more could there be to this wacky world?**))** – **K.K.**

Label: **Buddah/Buddah**
Date: **1969**

Includes: **Shake • Long In Fire • Quick Joey Small (Run Joey Run) • New York Woman • Up In The Air • I Got It Bad For You**

((All the Kasenetz-Katz stable of (largely non-existent) favourites come out to play. Ohio Express, the Music Explosion, the 1910 Fruitgum Company, Prof. Morrison's Lollipop and the Shadows Of Knight supposedly playing together and creating a bubblegum din that culminates in 'Quick Joey Small', a number so abrasive that someone must have slipped ground glass into the glutinous confection. **))** – **Ed.**

((All the greats combine together for a real scorcher – some of the snappiest numbers on record. An absolute must! A finger poppin', knee-shaker of an album. **))** – **K.K.**

110a

The Kasenetz-Katz Super Circus

'Quick Joey Small – I'm In Love With You'

111

The Velvet Underground

'The Velvet Underground And Nico'

Label: **Verve/Verve**
Date: **1967**

Includes: **I'm Waiting For The Man • Femme Fatale • Venus In Furs • Run Run Run • All Tomorrow's Parties • Heroin**

((Seminal decadence, influential stupidity, drugs and groovy death. **))** – **Ed.**

((Whilst California basked in an aura of innocence and optimism, the Velvet Underground dwelt on darker atmospheres – drugs, perversion, etc. – all within a shattering, discordant music combining garage-band chord sequences with the avant-garde. This approach proved to be ultimately closer to realism than the hippie San Francisco escapism and also related to the punk of ten years later. As relevant and powerful today as it ever was. **))** – **B.H.**

Musicians: **Lou Reed** (vocals, guitar) • **John Cale** (viola, bass, keyboards) • **Sterling Morrison** (guitar) • **Maureen Tucker** (drums) • **Nico** (vocals)

The Velvet Underground

'The Velvet Underground'

Label: MGM/MGM
Date: 1969

Includes: **Beginning To See The Light ● I'm Set Free ● The Murder Mystery ● Candy Says ● What Goes On ● Pale Blue Eyes ● Jesus**

❦Black and white – soft beauty and unspeakable horrors. 'Pale Blue Eyes', the gentlest of love songs, performed with seductive innocence; 'The Murder Mystery', the harshest of hate songs, performed with imperishable cynicism. A group out of anyone else's depth captured at their peak.❧ – **Ed.**

Musicians: As **The Velvet Underground And Nico,** without Nico

112

The Fugs

'Tenderness Junction'

Label: **Transatlantic/Reprise**
Date: 1968

Includes: **Turn On, Tune In, Drop Out ● Knock Knock ● Wet Dream ● War Song ● Dover Beach ● Fingers Of The Sun**

❦A New York Band who showed, with glorious O.T.T.-ness, their own particular brand of smart-ass cynicism and swimming. An essential LP for people into big hairy men with staring eyes who believed in a thing called 'armed love' and trusted Groucho rather than Karl Marx. 'Anarchists All!'❧ – **C.P.L. & F.K.**

Musicians: **Ken Weaver ● Tuli Kupfeberg ● Ed Sanders ●** and others

113

Frank Zappa

'Hot Rats'

Label: **Reprise/Bizarre**
Date: 1970

Includes: **Peaches En Regalia ● Willie The Pimp ● The Gumbo Variations ● It Must Be A Camel**

❦Frank's most accessible, least pretentious work, with superb musicians and Zappa reminding us of his own guitar skill.❧ – **C.W.**

Musicians: **Frank Zappa** (guitar, octave bass, percussion) ● **Ian Underwood** (keyboards, flute, clarinet, sax) ● **Sugar Cane Harris** (violin) ● **Jean Luc Ponty** (violin) ● **Max Bennett** (bass) ● **Captain Beefheart** (vocals) ● and others

113a

The Mothers Of Invention

'The Mothers Fillmore East June 1971'

Label: **Reprise/Bizarre**
Date: **1971**

Includes: **Little Home I Used To Live In** • **The Mud Shark** • **Latex Solar Beef** • **Willie The Pimp (parts 1 and 2)** • **Do You Like My New Car?** • **Happy Together** • **Tears Began To Fall**

❪❪It's almost impossible to decide which Zappa album to include – so many are brilliant – but when Frank and ex-Turtles Flo and Eddie cut the rug on this live outing of '200 Motels', no-one worth their lips could fail to have a yukking good time.**❫❫** – **C.P.L. & F.K.**

Musicians: **Frank Zappa** (guitar) • **Mark Volman** (vocals) • **Howard Kaylan** (vocals) • **Ian Underwood** (keyboards, woodwind) • **Aynsley Dunbar** (drums) • **Jim Pons** (bass, vocals) • **Bob Harris** (keyboards) • **Don Preston** (mini-moog)

114

Vanilla Fudge

'The Beat Goes On'

Label: **Atlantic/Atco**
Date: **1968**

Includes: **Sketch** • **Intro: The Beat Goes On** • **Eighteenth Century: Variations On A Theme By Mozart; Divertimento No 13 In F Major** • **Voices In Time** • **Merchant** • **The Game Is Over**

❪❪. . .'This album is people throughout the world, their ideas, beliefs, their emotions. We hold only the tools through which to express time through music.' So claim the boys, oozing sincerity, amidst the course of this, the ultimate CONCEPT album. Just what the 'concept' is, is hard to say: the Fudge's unique vision stretches across the entire history of music, politics, philosophy and sociology with unrivalled conceit, pretentiousness and arrogance. In short, this is probably the worst album ever made.

So why include it in a 'perfect collection', you ask? For three simple reasons. Firstly to remind one of the gross excesses to which rock has so often stretched. Secondly because this particular example of bombastic pomp is so *totally* ghastly that one can never be sure that it's not, in reality, a flawless masterpiece. And thirdly because I love it.**❫❫** – **Ed.**

Musicians: **Mark Stein** (keyboards) • **Vinnie Martell** (guitar) • **Tim Bogert** (bass) • **Carmine Appice**(drums)

115

The Godz

'Contact High With The Godz'

Label: **–/ESP**
Date: **1966**

Includes: **Turn On** • **Na Na Naa** • **Eleven** • **1+1=?** • **Squeak** • **White Cat Heat**

❪❪Whilst the intentions of the Vanilla Fudge remain unclear, there's no such confusion about New York 'band' the Godz. *Contact High* is a deliberate and highly successful attempt to create anti-music. Severely off-key vocals, squawking fiddle and other disturbing elements go into the production of an album that, whichever way you look at it, is definitively not mediocre. 'We don't give a good God-damn whether you dig it or not' proclaim the boys on the cover; and if you listen to it on headphones you go irreversibly mad. Dig it. **JJ** – **Ed.**

Musicians: **Jay Dillon** (psaltery) ● **Larry Kessler** (bass, violin) ● **Jim McCarthy** (guitar, plastic flute, harmonica) ● **Paul Thornton** (drums, guitar)

116

Iron Butterfly

'In-A-Gadda-Da-Vida'

Label: **Atlantic/Atco**
Date: **1968**

Includes: **Most Anything You Want** ● **Termination** ● **In-A-Gadda-Da-Vida**

JJSeventeen minutes of a stupid, sprawling, monotonous, mongoloid riff and a pseudo-foreign chant which became one of the biggest selling albums of all time. Okay, it's utterly banal and gross, but there's something about the elephantine, hypnotic organ, and Erik Brann's wrenching feedback entry after the metronomic drum 'solo' that I can't leave alone. A monumentally dumb masterwork. **JJ** – **Ed.**

Musicians: **Doug Ingle** (keyboards) ● **Erik Brann** (guitar) ● **Lee Dorman** (bass) ● **Ron Busjy** (drums)

117

Steppenwolf

'Steppenwolf Gold'

Label: **MCA/ABC**
Date: **1980**

Includes: **Born To Be Wild** ● **It's Never Too Late** ● **Rock Me** ● **Magic Carpet Ride** ● **The Pusher** ● **Screaming Nigh Hog**

JJLate Sixties hard rock for boys with leather-oriented motorcycle fantasies. At their worst, Steppenwolf were mundanely pseudo-political and musically pedestrian but at their best, as here, they kicked you along. Goldy McJohn's churning, percussive organ and Michael Monarch's active, slashing guitar create a peculiar drive that today's young, loud persons would do well to note. **JJ** – **Ed.**

Musicians: **John Kay** (vocals) ● **Goldy McJohn** (keyboards) ● **Michael Monarch** (guitar) ● **John Russell Morgan** (bass) ● **Larry Byrom** (guitar) ● **Nick St Nicholas** (bass) ● **George Biondo** (drums) ● **Jerry Edmonton** (drums) ● **Kent Henry** (guitar)

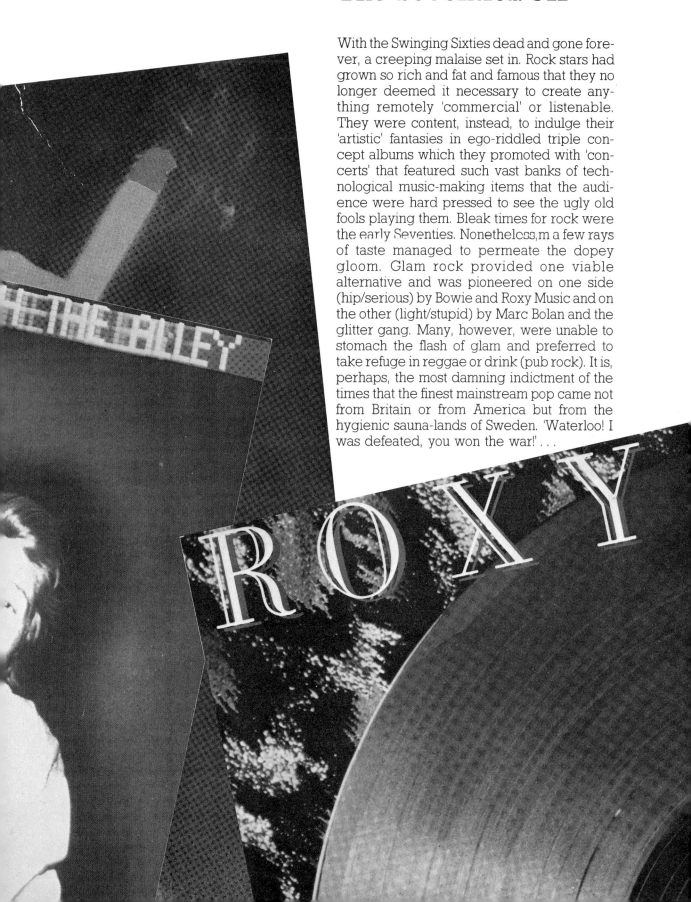

The Seventies/UK

With the Swinging Sixties dead and gone forever, a creeping malaise set in. Rock stars had grown so rich and fat and famous that they no longer deemed it necessary to create anything remotely 'commercial' or listenable. They were content, instead, to indulge their 'artistic' fantasies in ego-riddled triple concept albums which they promoted with 'concerts' that featured such vast banks of technological music-making items that the audience were hard pressed to see the ugly old fools playing them. Bleak times for rock were the early Seventies. Nonetheless, m a few rays of taste managed to permeate the dopey gloom. Glam rock provided one viable alternative and was pioneered on one side (hip/serious) by Bowie and Roxy Music and on the other (light/stupid) by Marc Bolan and the glitter gang. Many, however, were unable to stomach the flash of glam and preferred to take refuge in reggae or drink (pub rock). It is, perhaps, the most damning indictment of the times that the finest mainstream pop came not from Britain or from America but from the hygienic sauna-lands of Sweden. 'Waterloo! I was defeated, you won the war!' . . .

[118]

John Lennon

'John Lennon/Plastic Ono Band'

Label: **Apple/Apple**
Date: 1970

Includes: **Mother** • **Hold On** • **Isolation** • **Remember** • **Look At Me** • **God** • **My Mummy's Dead**

"Lennon's primal scream, tough and sick after all those years, spitting 'Don't believe in Beatles' at himself. Follow that, father.**"** – **Ed.**

[119]

Badfinger

'Straight Up'

Label: **Apple/Apple**
Date: 1972

Includes: **Money** • **Flying** • **I'd Die, Babe** • **Day After Day** • **Sometimes** • **It's Over**

"A marvellous album from one of the least hip bands of the early seventies. The debt to the latter-day Beatles is obvious, but Todd Rundgren's production highlights the band's passionate performance to such good effect that it really doesn't matter. Anyway, this is ten times better than *Let It Be* – no wonder poor Pete Ham bade farewell to this sunny world.**"** – **Ed.**

Musicians: **Pete Ham** (vocals, guitar) • **Tom**

Evans (vocals, bass) • **Joey Molland** (vocals, guitar) • **Mike Gibbins** (drums)

[120]

Richard And Linda Thompson

'I Want To See The Bright Lights Tonight'

Label: **Island/–**
Date: 1973

Includes: **When I Get To The Border** • **Withered And Died** • **I Want To See The Bright Lights Tonight** • **Down Where The Drunkards Roll** • **The End Of The Rainbow**

"A perfect example of English rock 'n' roll. Richard Thompson wrote a collection of literate, personal lyrics which fed off musical influences ranging from Jimmy Shand to Chuck Berry. Alternately joyous and despairing, Thompson's humanity shines through each song, affirming him a place as one of England's finest songwriters.**"** – **P.H.**

Musicians: **Richard Thompson** (vocals, guitar) • **Linda Thompson** (vocals) • with **Pat Donaldson** (bass) • **Timi Donald** (drums) • **John Kirkpatrick** (accordion) • **Trevor Lucas** (vocals) • **Simon Nicol** (guitar, vocals) • and others

[121]

Derek And The Dominoes

'Layla And Other Assorted Love Songs'

Label: **Polydor/Atco**
Date: 1971

Includes: **Layla** • **Have You Ever Loved A Woman** • **Nobody Knows You When You're Down And Out** • **Key To The Highway** • **Bell Bottom Blues** • **Little Wing**

"On which E.C. at last shows that he has more to offer the world than torpid, drippy guitar heroics.**"** – **G.D.**

Musicians: **Eric Clapton** (guitar, vocals) • **Carl Radle** (bass) • **Bobby Whitlock** (keyboards) • **Jim Gordon** (drums) • **Duane Allman** (guitar)

The Who

'Who's Next'

Label: **Track/Decca**
Date: 1971

Includes: **Baba O'Riley** • **Bargain** • **My Wife** • **Getting In Tune** • **Behind Blue Eyes** • **Won't Get Fooled Again**

❪❪The best rock LP of the Seventies.❫❫ – C.C.

Musicians: **Roger Daltrey** (vocals) • **Pete Townshend** (guitar, keyboards) • **John Entwhistle** (bass) • **Keith Moon** (drums)

122a

The Who

'Quadrophenia'

Label: **Track/MCA**
Date: 1973 (double)

Includes: **I Am The Sea** • **Cut My Hair** • **The Punk And The Godfather** • **I've Had Enough** • **5.15** • **Drowned** • **Bell Boy** • **The Rock**

❪❪One of the most consistently exciting groups of the Sixties and Seventies with an album as compelling as any of that era – a mini-history of the Who. Highlights among many are 'The Real Me' – with Entwhistle's 'lead bass' to the fore – and the brassy '5.15'. Forget 'Tommy' –

this is the Who's finest hour.❫❫ – M.H.

Musicians: As **Who's Next**

123

The Rolling Stones

'Exile On Main Street'

Label: Rolling Stones/Rolling Stones
Date: 1972 (double)

Includes: **Rocks Off** • **Tumbling Dice** • **Torn And Frayed** • **Happy** • **Ventilator Blues** • **Let It Loose** • **Shine A Light**

❪❪Their best album ever.❫❫ – C.C.

Musicians: **Mick Jagger** (vocals) • **Keith Richards** (guitar) • **Mick Taylor** (guitar) • **Bill Wyman** (bass) • **Charlie Watts** (drums) • and others

123a

The Rolling Stones

'Goats Head Soup'

Label: Rolling Stones/Rolling Stones
Date: 1973

Includes: **Dancing With Mr D.** • **100 Years Ago** • **Doo Doo Doo Doo Doo (Heartbreaker)** • **Silver Train** • **Star Star**

❪❪Their best album ever.❫❫ – Ed.

Musicians: As **Exile On Main Street**

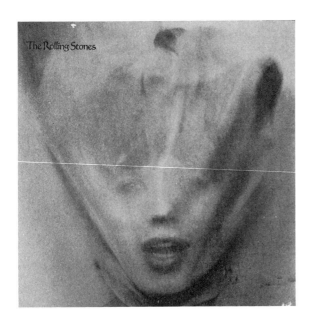

Musicians: **Bryan Ferry** (vocals, keyboards) •
Andy MacKay (sax) • **Phil Manzanera** (guitar)
• **Eno** (keyboards) • **Paul Thompson** (drums)
• **Eddie Jobson** (keyboards) • **Rik Kenton**
(bass) • **John Porter** (bass) • **John Gustafson**
(bass)

124

David Bowie

'The Rise And Fall Of Ziggy Stardust
And The Spiders From Mars'

Label: **RCA/RCA**
Date: 1972

Includes: **Five Years** • **It Ain't Easy** • **Starman**
• **Star** • **Ziggy Stardust** • **Suffragette City**

"A hearty dose of bisexual space rock never
hurt anyone. Especially if it changed the face
of pop music, which this did.**" – M.W.**

Musicians: **David Bowie** (vocals) • with **Mick
Ronson** (guitar) • **Trevor Bolder** (bass) • **Mick
'Woody' Woodmansey** (drums)

125

Roxy Music

'Greatest Hits'

Label: **Polydor/Atco**
Date: 1977

Includes: **Virginia Plain** • **Do The Strand** •
Editions Of You • **Love Is The Drug** • **The
Thrill Of It All** • **Street Life**

"For the Seventies' cleanest love songs –
words, music, voicings, the lot.**" – G.D.**

126

Gary Glitter

'Glitter'

Label: **Bell/Bell**
Date: 1972

Includes: **Rock And Roll Part 1** • **Baby Please
Don't Go** • **The Famous Instigator** • **I Didn't
Know I Loved You Till I Saw You Rock And
Roll** • **Rock On** • **Rock And Roll Part 2**

"With this debut album, the portly G.G. en-
capsulates the whole dumb ethic of the glitter
genre – moronic, metronomic beat, raucous
handclaps and gorilla shouts of 'Hey!' A record
touched with sub-human genius. 'I'm not much
good at music,' commented Gazbo at the
time.**" – Ed.**

"Gary at his greatest, proving glam rock was a
seminal influence on today's gays. The
greatest album ever made.**" – M.W.**

127

The Glitter Band

'Rock 'n' Roll Dudes'

Label: **Bell**/–
Date: **1975**

Includes: **Game's Up** ● **For Always And Ever** ● **All My Love** ● **Let's Get Together Again** ● **Do You Remember**

❟❟On excursions without their fat frontman (they never actually *played* on any of Gary's records), the Glitter Band proved themselves to be a more than capable pop band – and this is their greatest work. An amazing album, still in classic, early Seventies, glitter mould but veering towards a maturity and sophistication in songwriting and performance that's almost worrying. How a superb pop song like 'Game's Up' (also recorded by Hello) could fail to be a monster hit is one of the unexplained mysteries of the universe. ❟❟ – Ed.

Musicians: **John** ● **Gerry** ● **Tony** ● **Peter** ● **Harvey** ● **John**

128

Rod Stewart

'Every Picture Tells A Story'

Label: **Mercury**/Mercury
Date: **1971**

Includes: **Every Picture Tells A Story** ● **I'm Losing You** ● **Maggie May** ● **Mandolin Wind** ● **Reason To Believe** ● **Tomorrow Is A Long Time**

❟❟Rod at his most believable. 'Maggie May', songs by Dylan, Tim Hardin and Arthur Crudup as well as the works of Woody and Rod. ❟❟ – C.W.

Musicians: **Rod Stewart** (vocals) ● with: **Ron Wood** (guitar, bass) ● **Ian McLagen** (organ) ● **Mick Waller** (drums) ● **Danny Thompson** (bass) ● **Sam Mitchell** (guitar) ● and others.

129

ABBA

'Greatest Hits Volume 2'

Label: **Epic**/Atlantic
Date: **1979**

Includes: **Gimme, Gimme, Gimme (A Man After Midnight)** ● **Knowing Me, Knowing You** ● **Take A Chance On Me** ● **Money, Money, Money** ● **Dancing Queen** ● **Does Your Mother Know**

❟❟Clinical and heartless though the music of Sweden's secret weapon may be, there's no denying the immense skill with which it's assembled. However much one protests, they'll get you in the end. Cold but charming. ❟❟ – Ed.

Musicians: **Anni-Frid Lyngstad** ● **Agnetha Faltskog** ● **Benny Andersson** ● **Bjorn Ulvaeus**

130

Robert Palmer

'Sneakin' Sally Through The Alley'

Label: **Island**/Island
Date: **1974**

Includes: **Sailing Shoes** ● **Hey Julia** ● **Sneakin' Sally Thru The Alley** ● **Get Outside** ● **How Much Fun** ● **From A Whisper To A Scream**

❟❟White boy goes to New Orleans, meets Allen Toussaint and, against all the odds, succeeds where Jess Roden, Frankie Miller et al failed. The segued three-track opening to Side One is the steamiest piece of mood music this side of Marvin Gaye. And Palmer keeps tongue in cheek throughout. ❟❟ – M.H.

reaching new people with another universal language: reggae. **JJ** – **B.K.**

Musicians: **Bob Marley** (vocals, guitar) ● **Aston Barrett** (bass) ● **Carlton Barrett** (drums) ● **Touter** (keyboards) ● **Al Anderson** (guitar)

132

Toots And The Maytals

'Funky Kingston'

Label: **Trojan/–**
Date: **1976**

Includes: **Sit Right Down** ● **Pomp And Pride** ● **Louie Louie** ● **Daddy** ● **Funky Kingston** ● **I Can't Believe**

ffRock steddae for rudies and I know a good surname when I see one. **JJ** – **Ed.**

Musicians: **Toots Hibbert** ● **Hux Brown** ● **Jackie Jackson** ● **Paul Douglas** ● **Rad Bryan** ● **Rayleigh Gordon** ● **Jerry Mattias** ● **Winston Wright**

131

Bob Marley And The Wailers

'Natty Dread'

Label: **Island/Island**
Date: **1975**

Includes: **Natty Dread** ● **No Woman, No Cry** ● **So Jah Seh** ● **Bend Down Low** ● **Revolution**

ffMore than Jimmy Cliff or *The Harder They Come*, Marley's sound and this record broke Caribbean music out of its calypso stereotype,

132a

Toots And The Maytals

'In The Dark'

Label: **Dragon/–**
Date: **1974**

Includes: **Got To Be There** ● **In The Dark** ● **Having A Party** ● **Time Tough** ● **I See You**

ffThe ultimate party music of the pre-punk mid-Seventies. Authentic reggae backing melded to the soulful post-Otis vocals of Toots. Even John Denver's 'Country Roads' is redeemed to become a joyous anthem as West Virginia is overwhelmed by west Jamaica. **JJ** – **S.L.**

Musicians: As **Funky Kingston**

133

Mighty Diamonds

'Right Time'

Label: **Virgin/Virgin**
Date: **1976**

Includes: **Right Time** • **Why Me Black Brother Why** • **Gnashing Of Teeth** • **I Need A Roof** • **Have Mercy** • **Shame And Price** • **Natural Natty**

‖*The* classic JA vocal harmony group singing their most consistent collection of songs.**‖** – A.S.

Musicians: **Fitzroy Simpson** • **Lloyd Ferguson** • **Donald Shaw**

134

Bunny Wailer

'Blackheart Man'

Label: **Island/–**
Date: **1976**

Includes: **Battering Down Sentence** • **Armagedon** • **Fig Tree** • **Rasta Man** • **Dream Land**

‖Rich Rasta imagery, religious preoccupations and hymnal intensity make this one of reggae's warmest and most enriching albums.**‖** – M.P.

Musicians: **Bunny Wailer** • with: **Peter Tosh** (guitar) • **Robby Shakespeare** (bass) • **Carlton Barrett** (drums) • **Aston Barrett** (guitar) • and others

135

Dave Edmunds

'Get It'

Label: **Swan Song/Swan Song**
Date: **1977**

Includes: **Here Comes The Weekend** • **Ju Ju Man** • **Where Or When** • **Get It** • **Get Out Of Denver** • **Back To Schooldays**

‖The fact that Edmunds was able to record such an inspiring tribute to rock and roll without the soporific influences that prevailed in those trendy Seventies is a testimony to his talent and honesty as a performer.**‖** – M.M.

Musicians: **Dave Edmunds** (vocals, guitar, bass, keyboards) • with: **Terry Williams** (drums) • **Nick Lowe** (bass) • **Billy Rankin** (drums) • **Paul Riley** (bass) • **Billy Bremner** (guitar) • and others

136

Nick Lowe

'Jesus Of Cool' (US title 'Pure Pop For Now People', released on CBS with slightly altered track listing)

Label: **Radar/–**
Date: **1978**

Includes: **'Shake And Pop** • **Endless Sleep** • **Heart Of The City** • **Marie Provost** • **So It Goes** • **Little Hitler**

‖Married into a good family, likes a drink, a

touch sardonic, Nick displays a pleasing familiarity with no-nonsense beat music and stinging (stolen) hooks. Doggies dinners, healthy pumpers and dodgy old faves.**‖** – P.C.

‖So nice on drugs.**‖** – G.D.

137

David Bowie

'Station To Station'

Label: **RCA/RCA**
Date: **1976**

Includes: **Station To Station** ● **Golden Years** ●
Word On A Wing ● **TVC15** ● **Stay** ● **Wild Is
The Wind**

❪❪Even a non-devotee, such as myself, has to
admit that the self-styled Thin White Duke
came up with a cracker on this one. The compelling songs and gnashing guitar of Earl Slick
more than make up for 'The Laughing Gnome'
and other Bowie outrages. ❫❫ – **Ed.**

❪❪'Cos I like records with train noises. ❫❫ – **P.C.**

Musicians: **David Bowie** (vocals) ● with: **Earl
Slick** (guitar) ● **Carlos Alomar** (guitar) ● **Dennis Davies** (percussion) ● **George Murray**
(bass) ● **Roy Bittan** (keyboards) ● **Aynsley
Dunbar** (drums) ● and others

Musicians: **Marianne Faithfull** (vocals) ● with:
Jim Vuomo (sax, keyboards) ● **Guy Humphries**
(guitar) ● **Terry Stannard** (drums) ● **Darryl
Way** (violin) ● **Steve Winwood** (keyboards) ●
Steve York (drums) ● and others

138

Marianne Faithfull

'Broken English'

Label: **Island/Island**
Date: **1979**

Includes: **Broken English** ● **Brain Drain** ● **Guilt**
● **The Ballad Of Lucy Jordan** ● **What's The
Hurry** ● **Why D'Ya Do It**

❪❪What a croak in the throat meant in the late
Seventies. ❫❫ – **Ed.**

The Seventies/US

A new decade brought a mood of increased introspection and isolation, groups decaying into singer-songwriters who looked inside and back, exploring their musical heritage with varying degrees of success. Though the twin flags of revolt and cynicism were kept flying, albeit briefly, by the Velvet Underground, the Stooges and the MC5 (who sowed the seeds of heavy metal punk), it was country rockers, such as the Eagles, and pop egg-heads – Little Feat, Steely Dan – who enjoyed greater public acclaim. Pure-pop traditions were maintained by Todd Rundgren, Big Star and, later, Dwight Twilley and Tom Petty but few paid much attention as they were much too busy catching Saturday night fever and showing off their Travoltan pelvic techniques and Olivia Newton-John blusher in over-priced discos. Oui, c'est chic. New Jersey isn't (chic), however, and a dearth of disco activity centres in the area led to the emergence of the 'new Dylan' – Brooooooce!

139

Van Morrison

'Astral Weeks'

Label: **Warner Bros/Warner Bros**
Date: **1968**

Includes: **Cypress Avenue • Madam George • Sweet Thing • Astral Weeks**

"An unclassifiable classic. Morrison's searing blend of folk, blues, jazz, rock, R&B and Celtic mystery. An album that helped demolish the barriers which kept the music apart. Inscrutable and wholly wonderful.**"** – **P.H.**

"Atmospherically perfect.**"** – **C.C.**

Musicians: **Van Morrison** (vocals) • with: **Jay Berliner** (guitar) • **Richard Davis** (bass) • **Connie Kay** (drums) • **Warren Smith** (percussion) • **John Payne** (flute)

139a

Van Morrison

'Moondance'

Label: **Warner Bros/Warner Bros**
Date: **1970**

Includes: **And It Stoned Me • Caravan • Into The Mystic • Crazy Love • Moondance • Glad Tidings**

"Everything by Van Morrison possesses a special quality which others are only able to occasionally achieve.**"** – **J.T.**

"Cool and light like muesli breakfast.**"** – **P.W.**

Musicians: **Van Morrison** • with: **Jack Schroer** (sax) • **Colin Tillton** (sax and flute) • **Jeff Labes** (keyboards) • **John Platania** (guitar) • **John Klingberg** (bass) • **Gary Malaber** (drums) • and others

140

Tim Buckley

'Greetings From LA'

Label: **Warner Bros/Warner Bros**
Date: **1972**

Includes: **Move With Me • Night Hawkin' • Sweet Surrender • Devil Eyes • Make It Right • Get On Top • Hong Kong Bar**

"Buckley's most accessible and rockist album – aural eroticism from an esteemed white voice. 'Descriptive sex always appeals,' quipped Buckley shortly before his death.**"** – **Ed.**

"An unmatched voice.**"** – **G.D.**

Musicians: **Tim Buckley** (vocals, guitar) • **Joe Falsia** (guitar) • **Chuck Rainey** (bass) • **Ed Greene** (drums) • and others

141

Gene Clark

'No Other'

Label: **Asylum/Asylum**
Date: **1974**

Includes: **Life's Greatest Fool • No Other • Strength Of Strings • From A Silver Phial • Some Misunderstanding • The True One**

"There are two things that have to be sorted out right at the beginning. All the lyrics are appalling hippy dippy trash. Sample: 'And there's always light on the cosmic range/I am always high, I am always low.' The only reason that these awful words don't ruin *No Other* completely is that there are (almost literally)

hundreds of guitars all over the place. So every time a soppy conceit pops up, the crazed electric strings take its head off. The title track is a good case in point – a great mysterious swirl of voices and guitars propelled by quaintly named Allman Bro' Butch Trucks on drums. And the majority of the other independently minded arrangements win out over the 'we are all one' tish-tosh at the front of the mix too. And with sixteen musicians and nine singers accredited to the record, it's quite likely that Gene's still paying the studio bills – so do buy a copy.**JJ** – **P.C.**

ffVomit-inducing Zen Buddhism preaching – and the widest pair of flared trousers ever conceived by man – fail to overwhelm some utterly beautiful songs and arrangements. Jesse Ed Davis' guitar playing sets standards well nigh impossible to live up to. Warning: most of the music is so sweepingly spine-tingling, that gullible/susceptible ears might actually be converted to Gene's wonky point of view.**JJ** – **Ed.**

Musicians: **Gene Clark** (vocals, guitar) • **Lee Sklar** (bass) • **Jesse Ed Davis** (guitar) • **Richard Greene** (violin) • **Michael Utley** (keyboards) • **Butch Trucks** (drums) • and the entire population of California

142

The Velvet Underground

'Loaded'

Label: **Atlantic/Atlantic**
Date: **1971**

Includes: **Who Loves The Sun** • **Sweet Jane** • **New Age** • **Head Held High** • **Train Round The Bend** • **Oh! Sweet Nuthin'**

ffWhen the Velvet Underground's cynical, dark visions came together with an increased pop structure and greater studio discipline, it really *was* the beginning of a new age – or would have been if anyone had paid attention.**JJ** – **Ed.**

ffNew York's sleaziest cock a snook at the mellow Sixties with an answer to the Beatles' 'Here Comes The Sun' in a tune that asks 'Who needs it anyway?' A fine aural portrait of N.Y.'s pop-art, music crossover, ripping its own guts out in a glittering shower of methedrine crystals.**JJ** – **C.P.L. & F.K.**

Musicians: **Doug Yule** (keyboards, bass, drums, guitar, vocals) • **Sterling Morrison** (guitar) • **Lou Reed** (guitar, keyboards, vocals) • **Maureen Tucker** (drums)

143

Lou Reed

'Berlin'

Label: **RCA/RCA**
Date: **1973**

Includes: **Berlin** • **Lady Day** • **Caroline Says** • **The Kids** • **The Bed** • **Oh, Jim**

❪❪Quite simply his best solo album. A labour of decadent love. No one worth their tumeric can afford to be without an LP with lyrics like 'This is the room where she slashed her wrists/On that fateful night.' Which room did she slash them in on ordinary nights?❫❫ – **C.P.L. & F.K.**

Musicians: **Lou Reed** (vocals, guitar) • with: **Jack Bruce** (bass) • **Steve Hunter** (guitar) • **Allan MacMillan** (keyboards) • **Tony Levin** (bass) • **Aynsley Dunbar** (drums) • and (many) others

144

MC5

'Kick Out The Jams'

Label: **Elektra/Elektra**
Date: 1969

Includes: **Ramblin' Rose** • **Kick Out The Jams** • **Come Together** • **Rocket Reducer No. 64 (Rama Lama Fa Fa Fa)** • **Borderline** • **Motor City Is Burning**

❪❪Forget everything else, this is what inspired most punk bands; loud, bad, amphetamine rock by America's only really political pop anarchists. Brill!❫❫ – **M.W.**

❪❪Motor City heavy metal mixed with New Left politics and splendid (and naïve) idealism, this LP had ties to Grand Funk, Detroit, the Stooges, and was seminal punk.❫❫ – **B.K.**

Musicians: **Rob Tyner** (vocals) • **Wayne Kramer** (guitar) • **Fred 'Sonic' Smith** (guitar) • **Mike Davis** (bass) • **Dennis Thompson** (drums)

144a

MC5

'Back In The USA'

Label: **Atlantic/Atlantic**
Date: 1970

Includes: **High School** • **Back In The USA** • **American Ruse** • **Animal**

❪❪'Cos it hasn't got any slow ones.❫❫ – **P.C.**

Musicians: As **Kick Out The Jams**

145

Ry Cooder

'Into The Purple Valley'

Label: **Reprise/Reprise**
Date: 1971

Includes: **F.D.R. In Trinidad** • **Teardrops Will Fall** • **Denomination Blues** • **Money Honey** • **Taxes On The Farmer Feeds Us All** • **Vigilante Man** • **On A Monday**

❪❪On his second solo outing, Ry discovers America and paints a musical spectrum of many tunes. Plus – it fuckin' bops!❫❫ – **C.P.L. & F.K.**

Van Dyke Parks

'Discover America'

Label: **Warner Bros/–**
Date: **1970**

Includes: **Bing Crosby** ● **Riverboat** ● **Sailin' Shoes** ● **F.D.R. In Trinidad** ● **G-Man Hoover** ● **Jack Palance** ● **Be Careful** ● **The Four Mills Brothers**

❪❪Travelling back to pop's pre-history, the faceless session man returns with forgotten songs and styles and adds mysterious production touches that leave the few who are prepared to listen gasping 'How does he do that?' (and the rest who aren't, groaning '*Why* does he do that?') LP sells about fourteen copies, artist goes mad, tant pis.❫❫ – **Ed.**

❪❪L. A. wunderkind destroys career by recording an album of bizarre calypsos and thirties nostalgia with a steel band from Trinidad – contemporary to Cooder's *Purple Valley* voyage of musical discovery.❫❫ – **C.P.L. & F.K.**

147

Randy Newman

'Good Old Boys'

Label: **Warner Bros/Reprise**
Date: **1974**

Includes: **Rednecks** ● **Birmingham** ● **Kingfish** ● **Marie** ● **Every Man A King** ● **Louisiana 1927**

❪❪Never labelled as one but probably the best 'concept' album ever. Tasteful little digs at all colours, creeds, sizes, etc in the deep south of the USA.❫❫ – **P.P.**

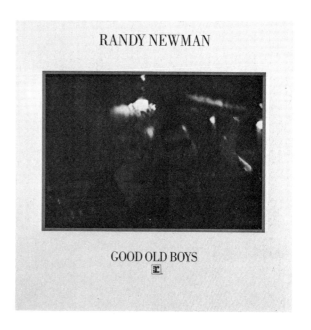

148

Gram Parsons

'GP'

Label: **Reprise/Reprise**
Date: **1973**

Includes: **Still Feeling Blue** ● **We'll Sweep Out The Ashes In The Morning** ● **Streets Of Baltimore** ● **That's All It Took** ● **She** ● **The New Soft Shoe**

❪❪The fragile, vulnerable voice of the poor little rich kid gropes its way through a superb selection of country melancholia and hoedown rock. The guitar of the almost legendary James Burton is on tip-top form and ex-Cricket Glen D. Hardin tickles the ivories with gusto. 'We'll Sweep Out The Ashes . . .' strikes a darkly prophetic note amidst the fun.❫❫ – **Ed.**

Musicians: **Gram Parsons** (vocals) ● **Emmylou Harris** (vocals) ● **James Burton** (guitar) ● **Glen D. Hardin** (keyboards) ● **Ronnie Tutt** (drums) ● **Byron Berlin** (violin) ● **John Conrad** (bass) ● **Alan Munde** (banjo) ● and others

[149]

John Fogerty

'The Blue Ridge Rangers'

Label: **Fantasy/Fantasy**
Date: 1973

Includes: **Jambalaya** ● **She Thinks I Still Care** ● **Workin' On A Building** ● **Please Help Me I'm Falling** ● **Have Thine Own Way, Lord** ● **Hearts Of Stone**

ɛɛLPs with solo artists playing all 34 instruments are usually the kiss of death. Men! John shows it can be done!ɹɹ – **P.P.**

[150]

Joni Mitchell

'Blue'

Label: **Reprise/Reprise**
Date: 1971

Includes: **Blue** ● **California** ● **My Old Man** ● **Carey** ● **Last Time I Saw Richard**

ɛɛOne of the few (possibly the only) female singer-songwriters of the era whose work has not dated horrendously with time. Whilst I defy anyone at all sensible to listen to, say, Melanie's scratch 'n' sniff album (let alone *smell* it) without feeling queasy, Joni causes no such embarrassment.ɹɹ – **N.W.**

Musicians: **Joni Mitchell** with **Russ Kunkel** (drums) ● **Stephen Stills** (guitar, bass) ● **James Taylor** (guitar, vocals) ● **Sneaky Pete Kleinow** (pedal steel)

[151]

The Beach Boys

'Surf's Up'

Label: **Reprise/Stateside**
Date: 1971

Includes: **Surf's Up** ● **Disney Girls** ● **Feel Flows** ● **Don't Go Near The Water** ● **Student Demonstration Time**

ɛɛDon Quixote's greatest tilts finds the 'Boys' shaking the sand out of their flip-flops and turning their attention to matters on the mainland. Obviously as a result of Dennis having been let out of the toilet by C. Manson, the B.B.s launch into a reworking of 'Riot On Cell Block No. 9' which is transferred from chokey to student politics. Then there's the beauty of 'Surf's Up' (featuring the words of madcap Van Dyke Parks) and 'Feel Flows'. *Surf's Up* also contains the odd, but vaguely forgiveable, weak moment courtesy of Mike Love who wreaks his usual California Cup Cake ecology/eagle beak havoc. That aside: give 'em a great big kiss.ɹɹ – **P.C.**

Musicians: **Carl Wilson** ● **Brian Wilson** ● **Dennis Wilson** ● **Mike Love** ● **Al Jardine** ● **Bruce Johnston** ● **Van Dyke Parks** ● and others

[152]

Little Feat

'Sailin' Shoes'

Label: **Warner Bros/Warner Bros**
Date: 1972

Includes: **Easy To Slip** ● **Cold, Cold, Cold** ● **Willin'** ● **Got No Shadow** ● **Cat Fever** ● **Texas Rose Cafe**

ɛɛBefore they became boringly funky and over-produced, Little Feat were recording marvellous songs that blended country, blues and R&B with imperishable bravura. Lowell George's words, Ritchie Hayward's drumming and the cake on the cover are just three of *Sailin' Shoes* starring elements. **JJ** – **Ed.**

ffOutside my hotel window is a neon sign that turns from red to green. It says 'Chop Suey' and 'Join the yeew esss mareeeeens'. **JJ** – **G.D.**

Musicians: **Lowell George** (vocals, guitar) • **Roy Estrada** (bass) • **Ritchie Hayward** (drums) • **Bill Payne** (keyboards)

Little Feat

'Waiting For Columbus'

Label: **Warner Bros/Warner Bros**
Date: **1978 (double)**

Includes: **Fat Man In The Bathtub** • **Oh Atlanta** • **Time Loves A Hero** • **Dixie Chicken** • **Sailin' Shoes** • **Tripe Face Boogie**

ffNearly ignored throughout their tragically short career, this rhythmic rock outfit put some of their spark into this live album. **JJ** – **B.K.**

ffA stunning synthesis of New Orleans funk, white rock and northern urban black blues. Lowell George never played better. **JJ** – **H.S.**

Musicians: **Lowell George** (vocals, guitar) • **Paul Barrere** (vocals, guitar) • **Ken Gradney** (bass) • **Ritchie Hayward** (drums) • **Bill Payne** (keyboards) • **Sam Clayton** (percussion, vocals) • and others

Steely Dan

'Can't Buy A Thrill'

Label: **Probe/ABC**
Date: **1972**

Includes: **Do It Again** • **Reeling In The Years** • **Dirty Work** • **Change Of The Guard** • **Only A Fool Would Say That**

ffJeff 'Skunk' Baxter's guitar playing rips through this platter and explodes into the cosmos as a lesson to Jimmy Page: 'Butt out kid, the throne's mine!' **JJ** – **M.W.**

Musicians: **Walter Becker** (keyboards, vocals) • **Donald Fagen** (bass, vocals) • **David Palmer** (vocals) • **Jeff 'Skunk' Baxter** (guitar) • **Denny Dias** (guitar) • **Jim Hodder** (drums)

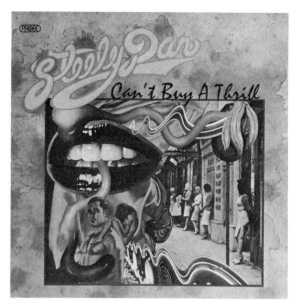

Steely Dan

'Countdown To Ecstasy'

Label: **ABC/ABC**
Date: **1973**

Includes: **Bodhisattva** • **The Boston Rag** • **Your Gold Teeth** • **Show Biz Kids** • **My Old School** • **King Of The World**

ffSteely precision, aluminium arrangements, precision tooled performances. Effective. **JJ** – **Ed.**

Musicians: As **Can't Buy A Thrill** without David Palmer

154

Crazy Horse

'Crazy Horse'

Label: **Reprise/Reprise**
Date: **1971**

Includes: **Beggar's Day ● Carolay ● I Don't Wanna Talk About It ● Gone Dead Train ● Downtown ● Dance, Dance, Dance**

❝The beautiful country/pop songs of Danny Whitten before succumbing to the needle. The sensational guitar work of boy wonder Nils Lofgren before succumbing to the trampoline.❞ – **Ed.**

Musicians: **Danny Whitten** (guitar, vocals) ● **Nils Lofgren** (guitar, vocals) ● **Jack Nitzsche** (keyboards) ● **Ralph Molina** (drums) ● **Billy Talbot** (bass)

155

Neil Young With Crazy Horse

'Zuma'

Label: **Reprise/Reprise**
Date: **1975**

Includes: **Don't Cry No Tears ● Danger Bird ● Lookin' For A Love ● Stupid Girl ● Cortez The Killer**

❝Neil Young has made all his best records with Crazy Horse for the simple reason that he needs a straightforward rock band to temper that ghastly melancholic whimsy which otherwise engulfs him. The title of the LP is a contraction of Montezuma – and the rape of the old world by the new is the theme. And as the old world is depicted as being festooned with pearls and loaded with cocaine, perhaps the new one had a point. The centrepiece of the album is 'Cortez The Killer', a gorgeously poignant guitar ballad which soars effortlessly above the apparent simplicity of its construction. As with all great guitarists, it's not so much that they play – it's the way they play them. Other stand outs include 'Stupid Girl' (yet another essay in ambiguous misogyny) and 'Drive Back'. Oh yes, and for all you CSN&Y fans who wondered why they never got back together (*after the seventy-fifth time, that is*' – Ed.) there's 'Through My Sails' – stop wondering.❞ – **P.C.**

Musicians: **Neil Young** (vocals, guitar) ● **Frank Sampedro** (guitar) ● **Billy Talbot** (bass) ● **Ralph Molina** (drums) ● **Tim Drummond** (bass) ● **Steve Stills** (guitar) ● **David Crosby** (whining) ● **Graham Nash** (further whining)

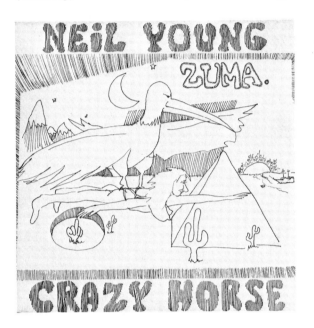

155a

Neil Young

'Live Rust'

Label: **Reprise/Reprise**
Date: **1979 (double)**

Includes: **Cinnamon Girl ● The Loner ● When You Dance I Can Really Love ● I Am A Child ● Like A Hurricane ● Tonight's The Night ● Comes A Time**

❝Young knocks the rust off his guitar with a selection of material from all stages of his career. In each case, the live performance is definitive – check the way he stretches out on 'Cortez The Killer' and 'Like A Hurricane' for the real meaning of *electric* guitar.❞ – **M.H.**

Musicians: **Neil Young** (vocals, guitar, keyboards) ● **Frank Sampedro** (guitar, keyboards) ● **Billy Talbot** (bass) ● **Ralph Molina** (drums)

156

Bruce Springsteen

'Born To Run'

Label: **CBS/Columbia**
Date: **1975**

Includes: **Thunder Road** ● **Tenth Avenue Freeze Out** ● **Night** ● **Born To Run** ● **She's The One** ● **Jungleland**

❝Superb songs, production, arrangements and timing.**❞** – C.C.

❝Power and sex in an urban setting. I think that Springsteen really *did* turn out to be the new Dylan.**❞** – H.S.

Musicians: **Bruce Springsteen** (vocals) ● with: **Clarence Clemons** (sax) ● **Garry Tallent** (bass) ● **Max Weinberg** (drums) ● **Roy Bittan** (keyboards) ● **Danny Federici** (keyboards) ● **Miami Steve Van Zandt** (guitar) ● **Vini 'Mad Dog' Lopez** ● and others

156a

Bruce Springsteen

'Darkness On The Edge Of Town'

Label: **CBS/Columbia**
Date: **1978**

Includes: **Badlands** ● **Prove It All Night** ● **Promised Land** ● **Racing In The Street**

❝The only major star the Seventies produced. Dismissed after the hype of *Born To Run* three years earlier, here Springsteen displayed a darker, brooding but nonetheless epic vision. Here was a rock 'n' roller who kept alive the spirit of Eddie Cochran and Phil Spector while tugging the spirit of rock into the Eighties.**❞** – P.H.

Musicians: As **Born To Run** (almost)

157

Big Star

'Radio City'

Label: **Stax/Ardent**
Date: **1971**
(UK release coupled with Big Star's first album, *Number 1 Record*)

Includes: **Way Out West** ● **What's Goin Ahn** ● **You Get What You Deserve** ● **Mod Lang** ● **Back Of A Car** ● **Daisy Glaze** ● **September Gurls**

❝Drawing on obvious influences – the Beatles, the Byrds – boy-genius Alex Chilton (ex-Box Tops vocalist) takes them somewhere else again with the most incongruous mixing techniques guitar pop has encountered. Voice, songs, guitar-work and general intentions make this the most playable album of the Seventies. Disgustingly ignored, Big Star should have been big stars. We are all guilty.**❞** – Ed.

Musicians: **Alex Chilton** (guitar, vocals) ● **Andy Hummel** (bass, vocals) ● **Jody Stephens** (drums) ● **Chris Bell** (guitar, vocals)

158

Nils Lofgren

'Nils Lofgren'

Label: **A&M/A&M**
Date: **1975**

Includes: **Be Good Tonight** ● **Back It Up** ● **If I Say It, It's So** ● **Keith Don't Go** ● **Can't Buy A Break** ● **Rock And Roll Crook** ● **Goin' Back**

❝One of the very few redeeming features of 1975. Boy wonder makes it to mature reality. With a pedigree stretching back to the original, ill-starred stars of Crazy Horse, through four albums with his own group Grin, this fellow had a lot to live up to. The winking, brandy-swigging figure on the cover appears confident enough and when the opening 'Be Good Tonight' fades into 'Back It Up', one can hear why. The expensive rhythm section works a treat, with Aynsley Dunbar particularly outstanding. The songs fizz past, deftly chronicling the mercurial lifestyle of a soft-centred hardcase, and the first side ends with Lofgren's plea to idol Keith Richard to cut out the naughties. The second side, meanwhile, continues in like-minded pop-rock vein until a neat arrangement of the old Goffin/King chestnut 'Goin' Back' gives Lofgren the chance to flex his pinkies on the piano.❞ – **P.C.**

Musicians: **Nils Lofgren** (vocals, guitar, keyboards) ● with: **Worrell Jones** (bass) ● **Aynsley Dunbar** (drums)

159

Todd Rundgren

'A Wizard, A True Star'

Label: **Bearsville/Bearsville**
Date: **1973**

Includes: **La La La Means I Love You** ● **International Feel** ● **Zen Archer** ● **Hungry For Love** ● **Is It My Name** ● **Cool Jerk**

❝There are times when only the outpourings of a complete nut-case will do. Put aside for one moment the abrasive craziness of *Trout Mask Replica* or *An Evening With Wild Man Fischer* and reach for the melodious, yet undeniably loopy *Wizard.* The cover itself is a hideously accurate portrayal of a mind in disarray and side one features all the aural grotesqueries you might expect from a boy-prodigy producer let loose in the studio without parental guidance. But hark! What is this wedged between the insane twitterings and buzzings? Songs of high quality, by George, and more than a few of them! By the second side, noises off have been given the bum's rush and by the middle of 'Cool Jerk', Todd is howling: 'Look at those guys looking at me like I'm a fool/But deep down inside they KNOW I'm cool!' The lad's got a point.❞ – **P.C.**

Musicians: **Todd Rundgren** (everything)

159a

Todd Rundgren

'Hermit Of Mink Hollow'

Label: **Bearsville/Bearsville**
Date: **1978**

Includes: **All The Children Sing** ● **Out Of Control** ● **Onomatopoeia** ● **Can We Still Be Friends** ● **You Cried Wolf** ● **Fade Away**

❝An all-too-rare example of Rundgren's commercial songwriting – a demo album of songs anyone could hit with. Love songs rub shoulders with nonsensical nursery rhymes, digs at

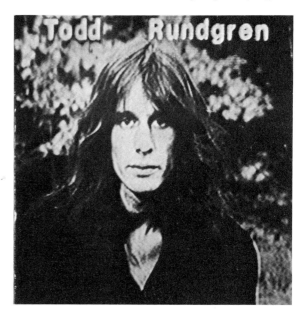

male chauvinism, social concern – *nothing* about the cosmos! With tunes like these, this guy could be a hip teen idol . . . if only . . . **))** – M.H.

Musicians: **Todd Rundgren** (the lot)

160

Dwight Twilley

'Twilley Don't Mind'

Label: **Shelter/Shelter**
Date: **1977**

Includes: **Twilley Don't Mind • Sleeping • Here She Comes • Looking For The Magic • That I Remember • Trying To Find My Baby**

((Inimitable rock 'n' roll pop music with vocal passion and urgency to bring on chills and hit nerves. 'Looking For The Magic' must be one of the most seductive pop love songs ever writ. And Dwight's face is so pretty!**))** – Ed.

Musicians: **Dwight Twilley** (vocals) • **Phil Seymour** (drums, vocals) • **Bill Pitcock** (guitar) • **Johnny Johnson** (bass)

161

Tom Petty And The Heartbreakers

'Tom Petty And The Heartbreakers'

Label: **Shelter/Shelter**

Date: **1977**

Includes: **Breakdown • The Wild One, Forever • Anything That's Rock 'N' Roll • Strangered In The Night • Luna • American Girl**

((Flash rock practitioner, not afraid to shut down the noise and let the hips do the talking, Petty rode shamelessly in on the new wave peddling some of the old. Impressive dynamics and tasteful economy lent weight to some fine tunes, one of which, 'American Girl', was rightly hailed as the best song never written by Roger ('Call me Jim') McGuinn.**))** – P.C.

Musicians: **Tom Petty** (vocals, guitar) • **Ron Blair** (bass) • **Stan Lynch** (drums) • **Mike Campbell** (guitar) • **Benmont Tench** (keyboards)

162

The Flamin' Groovies

'Teenage Head'

Label: **Kama Sutra/Kama Sutra**
Date: **1971**

Includes: **High Flyin' Baby • City Lights • Yesterday's Numbers • Teenage Head • Doctor Boogie • Whiskey Woman**

((The Flamin' Groovies have always been Big In Paris but don't let this put you off. One of the very few groups of the early Seventies to eschew gross guitar/keyboard gallimanfrey. Side one kicks off in a deceptively low-key shuffle with 'High Flyin' Baby' – and the perils of over-ambition are emphasised by some very slippery slide work. 'City Lights' sees the country hick pining for New York – 'where the planes shot that big monkey and they killed him'. Other highlights include the title track (don't know what it means but definitely classic) and 'Whiskey Woman' which builds subtly from quiet acoustic intro to a harder middle session courtesy of gracefully insinuated electric guitar before charging off the disc in crazed double time. The cover, incidentally, is a product of the notorious Groovies' undersell – the title appears nowhere on the front and the name of band only in tiny letters stencilled on a speaker cabinet in the group photo. Why?**))** – P.C.

"All's well that ends well." – Ed.

Musicians: **Roy Loney** (vocals) ● **Cyril Jordan** (guitar) ● **George Alexander** (bass) ● **Danny Mihm** (drums) ● **Tim Lynch** (guitar)

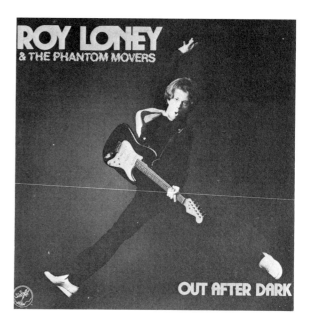

163

Roy Loney And The Phantom Movers

'Out After Dark'

Label: – /Solid Smoke
Date: **1979**

Includes: **Born To Be Your Fool** ● **Phantom Mover** ● **Neat Petite** ● **Return To Sender** ● **Rockin' In The Graveyard** ● **Scum City**

"The best album the Flaming Groovies never made. Whilst Loney's old band were dressing up as the Kink Beatles and desperately thrashing around for direction with a lot of wonky old cover versions (and, to give them their due, the occasional gem), Roy was content to continue along the rock 'n' roll path. His love/hate relationship with the form shines through this collection of speedy, electric rock mania. A wizard – a true cult hero. (Makes Dave Edmunds look like a stoutish wimp.)" – Ed.

Musicians: **Roy Loney** (vocals, guitar) ● **Danny Mihm** (drums) ● **Larry Lea** (guitar) ● **James Ferrell** (guitar) ● **Maurice Tani** (bass) ● **Nick Buck** (keyboards)

164

Blue Oyster Cult

'Spectres'

Label: **CBS/Columbia**
Date: **1977**

Includes: **Godzilla** ● **Death Valley Nights** ● **Fireworks** ● **Celestial The Queen** ● **Goin' Through The Motions** ● **I Love The Night**

"Wherin the Cult go for a wider public. Having thrown off the yoke of the outrageous lyrics which Murray Krugman and Sandy Pearlman used to foist on them, the group gets down to some lyrical heavy metal. This is the sound of dinosaurs *singing*. Yet under the layers of cornball posturing and braggadocio, moves something moving; shed a tear for old Drac in 'Nosferatu', goose pimple to the strains of ghostly love in 'I Love The Night', blubber horribly over 'Death Valley Nights' – this is a SAD record for Christ's sake . . . In the unlikely event of this being insufficient you can still snigger at 'Godzilla' or gloat over the fathomless vulgarity of 'The Golden Age Of Leather'. Heavy metal music with wit and brains, Magic." – P.C.

Musicians: **Eric Bloom** (vocals, guitar) ● **Joe Bouchard** (vocals, bass) ● **Donald Roeser** (guitar, vocals) ● **Albert Bouchard** (drums, vocals) ● **Allen Lanier** (keyboards, vocals)

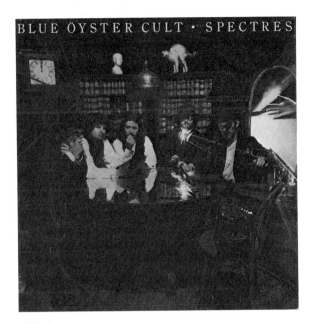

165

Sly and The Family Stone

'There's A Riot Going On'

Label: **Epic/Epic**
Date: **1971**

Includes: **Thankyou For Talking To Me, Africa • Brace And Strong • Africa Talks To You (The Asphalt Jungle) • Runnin' Away • Family Affair**

❝Funk shutdown. A devastating portrayal of urban decay and personal turmoil – bad riots in the streets, bad drugs in the veins. The 'songs' are dragged kicking and screaming from the grooves – this is not party music. The two hits from the album – 'Runnin' Away' and 'Family Affair' might initially give the wrong impression but first listen to the words. The rest are hardly songs at all – more a soundtrack for oblivion.❞ – P.C.

Musicians: **Sly Stone** (vocals, keyboard, guitar) • **Freddie Stone** (guitar) • **Rose Stone** (vocals) • **Gregg Errica** (drums) • **Jerry Martini** (sax) • **Cynthia Robinson** (horns) • **Larry Graham** (bass) • and others

166

Jackson Five

'Greatest Hits'

Label: **Tamla Motown/Motown**
Date: **1972**

Includes: **I Want You Back • ABC • Never Can Say Goodbye • Sugar Daddy • I'll Be There • The Love You Gave • Who's Lovin' You**

❝Disco/soul bippity-bop music for tots and grown-ups too.❞ – Ed.

Musicians: **Jackie (Sigmund) • Marlon • Tito • Jermaine • Michael Jackson**

167

The Staples Singers

'Bealtitude: Respect Yourself'

Label: **Stax/Stax**
Date: **1972**

Includes: **Respect Yourself • I'll Take You There • We The People • Are You Sure • I'm Just Another Soldier**

❝Smooth and seductive gospel/soul with an undefinable undertow.❞ – P.P.

Musicians: **Mavis • Cleo • Yvonne • Roebuck 'Pops' Staples**

168

Al Green

'Greatest Hits'

Label: **London/Hi**
Date: **1975**

Includes: **Sha La La** ● **I'm Still In Love With You** ● **Let's Stay Together** ● **Let's Get Married** ● **Tired Of Being Alone**

ΙΙA matchless voice, some impeccable drumming and the inimitable tone of Charlie Hodges economic organ.**ΙΙ** – P.P.

Musicians: **Al Green** (vocals) ● **Charlie Hodges** (keyboards) ● **Al Jackson** (drums) ● **Leroy Hodges** (bass) ● **Teenie Hodges** (guitar) ● **Howard Grimes** (drums) ● and others

169

Michael Jackson

'Off The Wall'

Label: **Epic/Epic**
Date: **1979**

Includes: **Don't Stop Till You Get Enough** ● **Rock With You** ● **Off The Wall** ● **Girlfriend** ● **She's Out Of My Life** ● **It's The Falling In Love**

ΙΙWonderfully precision disco that pinpointed Saturday NIght Fever!**ΙΙ** – I.B.

170

Chic

'Risque'

Label: **Atlantic/Atlantic**
Date: **1979**

Includes: **Good Times** ● **My Forbidden Lover** ● **My Feet Keep Dancing** ● **Can't Stand To Love You** ● **What About Me**

ΙΙEndlessly listenable, endlessly danceable – still their best LP.**ΙΙ** – A.S.

Musicians: **Bernard Edwards** (bass) ● **Nile Rodgers** (guitar) ● **Tony Thompson** (drums) ● **Raymond Jones** (keyboards) ● **Robert Sabine** *(keyboards)* ● **Sammy Figueroa** (percussion)

• **Andy Schwartz** (percussion) • and a cast of singers, tap dancers and sundry artistes

Sheila And B. Devotion

'King Of The World'

Label: **Carrere**/ –
Date: **1980**

Includes: **Spacer** • **Mayday** • **Charge Plates And Credit Cards** • **King Of The World** • **Cover Girls**

ʜSheila's indecipherable French accent combines with the songs and arrangement of Chic Organization directors Nile Rodgers and Bernard Edwards to produce a disco album that is not only 'danceable' but infinitely listenable to boot. The guitar solo on 'Spacer' causes a riot in the brain if listener is unprepared. ʜ – **Ed.**

Musicians: **C'est Chic**

Punk And The Eighties

'I am eleven years old and when I saw those people in the 'Mirror' with safety pins through their nostrils it made me feel sick. If I saw them I'd tell them how dangerous it is and how stupid it looks.' – Letter, *Daily Mirror,* 1976

The American backlash came first – in fact it had always been there. For throughout the Seventies occasional protesting voices – from the MC5 to Iggy and the Stooges, from Lou Reed to the New York Dolls – had raised snarls at the complacencies of rock. But no-one paid much heed. By 1976, an alternative 'punky' scene had grown up in New York; the Ramones, Patti Smith, Television and remnants of the Dolls were playing to clubs packed with misfits and losers. But it was in England, where the musical vista had become even more sterile, that punk was to find its essential voice. Johnny Rotten and his spiky-topped chums appeared on telly and one irate father was moved to kicking his set to pieces. It was like the Rolling Stones all over again but more so. The punk surge flowed into the new wave and thence toward post-industrial gloom and new romanticism. Inevitably, nothing *really* changed; the majors remained in control. But at least pop music was back in the hands of the young where it belonged. And at least no-one would ever again dare to include an extended drum solo on album . . . Or would they? . . .

[172]

The Modern Lovers

'The Modern Lovers'

Label: **Beserkley/Berserkley**
Date: **1976**

Includes: **Roadrunner** • **Old World** • **Pablo Picasso** • **She Cracked** • **Hospital** • **Modern World**

❝Before Jonathan Richman started believing he was a little insect and an ice-cream man, he thought he was the Velvet Underground. And for a few moments in 1971 (the album was released five years after it had been recorded) he half was. The other half was Fabian, or similar teen-dream boy-next-door-but-one. So instead of warbling sweet nothin's to his baby on the beach, he has to deliver his romantic sentiments to the hospital bed where she lies. The thick-tin sound of 'I'm Waiting For The Man' meets the white-washed wood of New England with intriguing results.❞ – **Ed.**

Musicians: **Jonathan Richman** (vocals, guitar) • **Jerry Harrison** (keyboards, guitar) • **Ernie Brooks** (bass) • **David Robinson** (drums)

[173]

Iggy Pop And James Williamson

'Kill City'

Label: **Radar/Bomp**
Date: **1978**

Includes: **Kill City** • **Beyond The Law** • **I Got Nothin'** • **Consolation Prizes** • **Lucky Monkeys**

❝After the self-destruct obsessions and power-drill gonzo-babble of the Stooges, *'Kill City'*, recorded in 1975, after *'Raw Power'*, came as a monumental surprise. It's vicious, hard, relentless, etc but at the same time it's controlled and directional. Perfect punk songs, a savage but strangely disciplined vocal performance from da Ig, searing sax passages and the burning guitar of Williamson. Hard-edged exhiliration and *real* raw power.❞ – **Ed.**

Musicians: **Iggy Pop** (vocals) • **James Williamson** (guitar) • **Scott 'Try' Thruston** (keyboards) • **Brian Glascock** (drums, percussion) • **Steve Tranio** (bass) • **Tony Sales** (bass) • **Hunt Sales** (drums) • and others

[174]

The Ramones

"The Ramones'

Label: **Sire/Sire**
Date: **1976**

Includes: **Blitzkreig Bop** • **Beat On The Brat** • **Judy Is A Punk** • **Chain Saw**

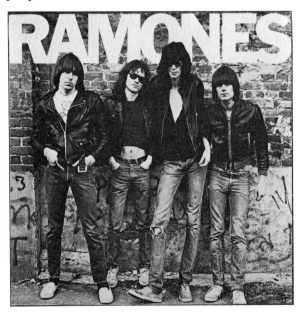

ΙΙOozing out of New York at just the right moment, all ripped jeans and rotting teeth, the Ramones injected a welcome note (just the one, of course) of deadpan humour into the punk tirade to be. Peanuts for Punks.**ΙΙ** – P.C.

Musicians: **Joey Ramone** (vocals) • **Johnny Ramone** (guitar) • **Dee Dee Ramone** (bass) • **Tommy Ramone** (drums)

175

Patti Smith

'Horses'

Label: **Arista/Arista**
Date: **1975**

Includes: **Gloria** • **Redondo Beach** • **Free Money** • **Kimberly** • **Break It Up** • **Land** • **Elegie**

ΙΙPatti the poetess made a lasting impression with this venomous debut that eliminated fence-sitting at a stroke. The longer pieces are occasionally prone to the Morrison syndrome (Jim not Van) but the majority prove that the lady's no tramp. The acceptable face of punk feminism with Lenny Kaye's squawling guitar to boot.**ΙΙ** – Ed.

Musicians: **Patti Smith** (vocals) • **Lenny Kaye** (guitar) • **Richard Sohl** (piano) • **Ivan Kral**

(guitar, bass) • **Jay Dee Daugherty** (drums) • **Tom Verlaine** (guitar) • **Allen Lanier** (guitar)

176

Sex Pistols

'Never Mind The Bollocks!... Here's The Sex Pistols!'

Label: **Virgin/Warner Bros**
Date: **1978**

Includes: **Anarchy In The UK** • **God Save The Queen** • **Pretty Vacant** • **Holidays In The Sun** • **EMI** • **Liar**

ΙΙThe only proper album from the only proper band of the Seventies. Despite Rotten's threat that the Pistols were out to destroy rock 'n' roll, they were, ironically, its greatest benefactor during the decade. The Pistols took rock away from the stadiums and light shows back to its roots. They created a movement, the repercussions of which are still being felt five years on.**ΙΙ** – P.H.

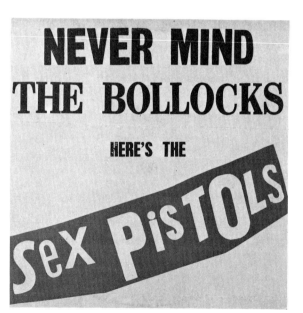

ΙΙBack to basics – and not before time.**ΙΙ** – C.C.

ΙΙAs far as Punk Ethos is concerned, this album says it all. Music for Thatcher's Eighties.**ΙΙ** – H.S.

ΙΙA monstrous conceit is captured at its nadir

by this bouncy, sing-along classic. And everything else they say about it. **))** – **M.W.**

((An exercise in sustained good taste. **))** – **P.C.**

((Where's the money? **))** – **Ed.**

Musicians: **John(ny) Lydon (Rotten)** (vocals) • **Steve Jones** (guitar) • **Sid Vicious** (John Ritchie) (bass) • **Paul Cook** (drums)

177

The Clash
'London Calling'

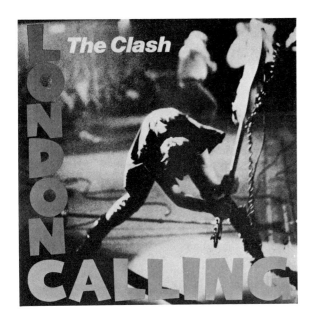

Label: **CBS/Epic**
Date: **1979 (double)**

Includes: **London Calling** • **Spanish Bombs** • **Clampdown** • **Lost In The Supermarket** • **The Guns Of Brixton** • **Revolution Rock** • **Jimmy Jazz**

((A double album of clanking musical fervour and articulate working class humanitarianism. At once worthy, exciting and grand, this sees the Clash extending punk's limited concerns and investing other musical vehicles with their bulldozer spirit. **))** – **M.P.**

Musicians: **Joe Strummer** (vocals, guitar) • **Mick Jones** (guitar) • **Paul Simonon** (bass) • **Nicky 'Topper' Headon** (drums)

178

Television
'Marquee Moon'

Label: **Elektra/Elektra**
Date: **1977**

Includes: **I See No Evil** • **Venus De Milo** • **Marquee Moon** • **Elevation** • **Guiding Light** • **Torn Curtain**

((An extraordinary feat. The guitars of Tom Verlaine and Richard Lloyd cross and contrast, each note planned to fit, while the rhythm section of Ficca and Smith remains dry and immaculate throughout – they punctuate not only the music but the lyrics too. As for Verlaine's songs, they're chilling, gripping, haunting and lots of other words I can't think of. The nearest rock ever got to an Austrian spook movie in black and white. **))** – **Ed.**

((One of the great American rock and roll bands of all time and one of the most (commercially at least) underrated. **))** – **A.S.**

Musicians: **Tom Verlaine** (guitar) • **Richard Lloyd** (guitar) • **Fred Smith** (bass) • **Billy Ficca** (drums)

178a

Television

'Adventure'

Label: **Elektra/Elektra**
Date: **1978**

Includes: **Glory** • **Days** • **Foxhole** • **Carried Away** • **The Fire** • **Ain't That Nothin'**

ʞʞTom Verlaine's ability to tame dissonant guitar licks into coherent, lyrical whatsits was established beyond all doubt by this product. Magic.ʝʝ – **M.W.**

Musicians: As **Marquee Moon**

179

Talking Heads

'Fear Of Music'

Label: **Sire/Sire**
Date: **1979**

Includes: **Heaven** • **Life During Wartime** • **Memories Can't Wait** • **Cities** • **Electric Guitar** • **Drugs**

ʞʞThe Heads on the block, neuroses exposed like bared nerve endings, a week without sleep, grim tension sliding into soaring melody, all this and more. The very best Talking Heads record and silly old Brian Eno's finest moment. Who can resist 'Drugs' with its bird noises recorded at the 'Lone Pine Koala Sanctuary', Brisbane, Australia? Not me but then: 'I'm mad and that's a fact'.ʝʝ – **P.C.**

ʞʞFor 'Heaven is a place where nothing ever happens,' the most beautiful and chilling line in the English language.ʝʝ – **Ed.**

Musicians: **David Byrne** (vocals, guitar) • **Jerry Harrison** (guitar, keyboards) • **Tina Weymouth** (bass) • **Chris Frantz** (drums) • **Brian Eno** (treatments)

180

Iggy Pop

'The Idiot'

Label: **RCA/RCA**
Date: **1977**

Includes: **Sister Midnight** • **Nightclubbing** • **China Girl** • **Dum Dum Boys** • **Mass Production**

ʞʞOn which David Bowie comes to the rescue of a fallen anti-star and invests him with renewed hip – and punk (this is 1977) – credibility. And on which Iggy repays any debt with a compelling, disturbing performance. The mind-bashing self (and everyone else) hatred of previous years is replaced by space and haunting things. Listen more closely and James Jewel Osterburg is revealed as the caustic wit he has become – 'The first time I saw the dum dum boys/I was fascinated/They just stood in front of the old drug store/I was most impressed/No one else was impressed/

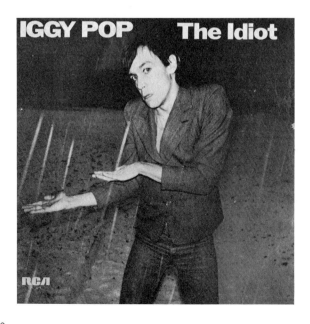

Not at all'. **))** – **Ed.**

Musicians: **Iggy Pop** (vocals) ● **Carlos Alomar** (guitar) ● **Ricky Gardner** (guitar) ● **Tony Sales** (bass) ● **Hunt Sales** (drums) ● **David Bowie** (keyboards, vocals)

180a

Iggy Pop
'Lust For Life'

Label: **RCA/RCA**
Date: **1978**

Includes: **Success** ● **Lust For Life** ● **The Passenger** ● **Some Weird Sin** ● **Sixteen** ● **Turn Blue** ● **Neighborhood Threat** ● **Tonight**

((Lighter, and less brooding than *The Idiot,* this is Iggy's most accessible, rocky and 'happy' (despite some black japes) LP. Whilst all around him turn gloomy, J.J. does the floor kiss, cheers up and jumps like a frog. **))** – **Ed.**

((For the 'Oh shit!' refrain in 'Success'. **))** – **G.D.**

Musicians: As **The Idiot**

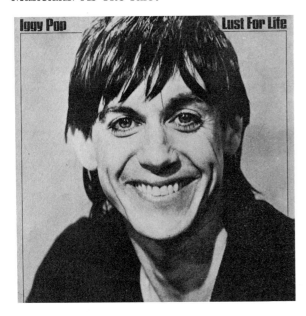

181

Joy Division
'Unknown Pleasures'

Label: **Factory/–**
Date: **1979**

Includes: **Disorder** ● **Day Of The Lords** ● **Candidate** ● **She's Lost Control** ● **I Remember Nothing**

((Martin Hannett, the producer of this LP, once told me that he had a dream around 1970 in which he saw a band climb on stage in a church hall and perform wonderful songs. In 1977, whilst mixing for a band in Salford, his dream turned to reality. The band was Joy Division. Whatever the transcendental ontology of the group, their importance could hardly have been greater if they had arrived in a fiery chariot. As for influence, it has been conservatively estimated that on any particular night in 1981, the mobile British punter would be able to choose between several thousand Joy Division clones if seeking live entertainment. This is the album that made their musical reputation as they add depression, anguish and contemplation to the aggression and frustration that characterised the emotional repertoire of early punk. **))** – **S.L.**

Musicians: **Ian Curtis** (vocals) ● **Bernard Albrecht** (guitar) ● **Peter Hook** (bass) ● **Stephen Morris** (drums)

182

Echo And The Bunnymen
'Crocodiles'

Label: **Korova/–**
Date: **1980**

Includes: **Rescue** • **Villiers Terrace** • **All That Jazz** • **Going Up** • **Pictures On My Wall** • **Monkeys**

❝The linear funk of the rhythm section, the atmospheric haze of the guitar, the meaningless grip of the lyrics and the impetuous structure of the songs make *Crocodiles* the first essential British post-punk album.**❞** – **N.W.**

Musicians: **Ian McCulloch** (vocals, guitar) • **Will Sergeant** (guitar) • **Les Pattison** (bass) • **Pete De Freitas** (drums)

183

The Cure

'Faith'

Label: **Fiction/–**
Date: **1981**

Includes: **The Holy Hour** • **Primary** • **All Cats Are Grey** • **The Funeral Party** • **The Drowning Man** • **Faith**

❝Scratch beneath the surface of the Cure's grey, bleak industrial despair and discover optimism amidst the post-punk guitar wall o' sound. Dynamic tension, atmospherics, and intangible je ne sais quois single the Cure out from the heap of Eighties pop boys gone serioso. **❞** – **N.W.**

Musicians: **Robert Smith** (vocals, guitar, keyboards) • **Simon Gallup** (bass) • **Laurence Tollhurst** (drums)

184

Elvis Costello

'Trust'

Label: **F-Beat/Columbia**
Date: **1981**

Includes: **Clubland** • **Watch Your Step** • **Luxembourg** • **From A Whisper To A Scream** • **Different Finger** • **Shot With His Own Gun**

❝Conclusive proof, if any doubted it, that here was the best new songwriter to emerge in Britain in years. It was the new wave that brought him to the fore but Costello would have been a star whatever the fashion. Here, his fifth album, the scope and depth of his songs is breathtaking. **❞** – **P.H.**

Musicians: **Elvis Costello** (guitar, vocals) • **Bruce Thomas** (bass) • **Peter Thomas** (drums) • **Steve Naive** (keyboards)

185

Graham Parker And The Rumour

'Squeezing Out Sparks'

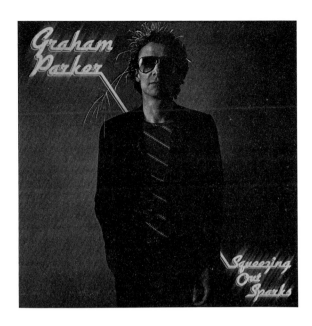

Label: Vertigo/Arista
Date: 1979

Includes: Nobody Hurts You • You Can't Be Too Strong • Passion Is No Ordinary Word • Saturday Nite Is Dead • Don't Get Excited

❪❪Parker's peak, on which he walks all over accusations of derivative R&B-recycling and creates a personal, powerful and passionate statement to end the Seventies. When he urges and receives maximum commitment from his backing band, as in 'Discovering Japan', the momentum just carries you away – no question.**❫❫** – **M.H.**

Musicians: **Graham Parker** (vocals) • **Brinsley Schwarz** (guitar) • **Bob Andrews** (keyboards) • **Martin Belmont** (guitar) • **Andrew Bodnar** (bass) • **Steve Goulding** (drums)

186

Blondie

'The Best Of Blondie'

Label: Chrysalis/Chrysalis
Date: 1982

Includes: Heart Of Glass • Denis • Picture This • Hanging On The Telephone • Rapture • Rip Her To Shreds

❪❪Blondie were always going to go platinum – their secret was they didn't care. Old enough to know better, they kept their heads when their contemporaries were comprised by fame and riches. As they grew famous, their public persona was orchestrated; Debbie no longer confessed to liking smack and stopped rolling demented on the stage, but their private intelligence and stability remained. Their albums moved from Fifties sci-fi hysteria to polished analgesics but their singles would have been classics in any era. Debbie Harry's precise but slurred voice floats above Clem Burke's driving beat, everything else fitting together like a Swiss watch. Pure perfection. How could they do it and remain real people?**❫❫** – **S.L.**

Musicians: **Debbie Harry** (vocals) • **Chris Stein** (guitar) • **Clem Burke** (drums) • **Nigel Harrison** (bass) • **Jimmy Destri** (keyboards)

187

The B-52's

'The B-52's'

Label: Island/Island
Date: 1979

Includes: Planet Claire • 52 Girls • Rock Lobster • Lava • Hero Worship • Dance This Mess Around

❪❪'We were at a party, his ear lobe fell in the deep' is a fair sample of the delightful gibberish purveyed by these wonderful bobby soxers from Athens, Georgia. Characteristics:

beehive hairdos, pencil moustaches, tacky accessories, open tunings – in short Annette and Fabian and Frankie's real beach party. Favourite cheese: limburger. Favourite tracks: 'Dance This Mess Around', 'Lava' (check for sexual metaphor)/'52 Girls' (count 'em!) and, not forgetting all you Pet Clark fans out there, 'Downtown'. Favourite B52: go on, you choose! **))** – **P.C.**

Musicians: **Kate Pierson** (vocals, keyboards) • **Fred Schneider** (vocals, keyboards) • **Keith Strickland** (drums) • **Cindy Wilson** (vocals, percussion) • **Ricky Wilson** (guitar)

188

The Pretenders
'The Pretenders'

Label: **Real Records/Sire**
Date: **1979**

Includes: **Stop Your Sobbing** • **Kid** • **Brass In Pocket** • **Private Life** • **The Wait** • **Up The Neck** • **Space Invader**

((A blockbuster of a debut album in which Chrissie Hynde shot her creative bolt it seems. Hope she proves me wrong, but these twelve tracks will be hard to beat for their energy and eclecticism. **))** – **M.H.**

Musicians: **Chrissie Hynde** (vocals, guitar) • **Pete Farndon** (bass) • **James Honeyman-Scott** (guitar, keyboards, vocals) • **Martin Chambers** (drums)

189

The Buzzcocks
'Singles: Going Steady'

Label: **United Artists/United Artists**
Date: **1979**

Includes: **Orgasm Addict** • **What Do I Get** • **Ever Fallen In Love?** • **Everybody's Happy Nowadays** • **Oh Shit!** • **Autonomy**

((Soaring, sweeping pop songs encapsulating fleeting joys and dirty emotions. All spirit and energy (and a guitar sound you could lean on). **))** – **M.P.**

Musicians: **Pete Shelley** (vocals, guitar) • **Steve Diggle** (guitar) • **Steve Garvey** (bass) • **John Maher** (drums)

190

The Undertones
'Hypnotised'

Label: **Sire/Sire**
Date: **1980**

Includes: **More Songs About Chocolate And Girls** • **Wednesday Week** • **My Perfect Cousin** • **There Goes Norman** • **See That Girl** • **Tearproof** • **What's With Terry**

((Sparkling adolescent pop of the simplest and most refreshing kind. **))** – **M.P.**

Musicians: **Fergal Sharkey** (vocals) • **John O'Neill** (guitar) • **Damian O'Neill** (guitar) • **Mickey Bradley** (bass) • **Billy Doherty** (drums)

191

The Soft Boys
'Underwater Moonlight'

Label: **Armageddon/–**
Date: **1980**

Includes: **Kingdom Of Love** • **Positive Vibrations** • **I've Got The Hots For You** • **Queen Of Eyes** • **Insanely Jealous** • **Underwater Moonlight**

((Harmonies and humour; melodies and caustic wit; guitar solos; sitar solos. There was just no way that this album could please the critics within 1980's cold, industrial context. It exuded warmth at a time when gloom and clanking electronic dirges were the accepted norm. But time will show that *Underwater Moonlight* was a gem of Sixties-inspired pure pop. **))** – Ed.

((A triumph of musical talent over fashion and fads – the thin production apart, this album is a minor classic. Yesterday's sound today – oh boy, totally fab! **))** – N.C.

Musicians: **Robyn Hitchcock** (guitar, vocals) ● **Kimberley Rew** (guitar, vocals) ● **Matthew Seligman** (bass) ● **Morris Windsor** (drums, vocals) ● and others

192

The dB's

'Repercussion'

Label: **Albion/Albion**
Date: **1982**

Includes: **Living A Lie** ● **Amplifier** ● **Ask For Jill** ● **I Feel Good (Today)** ● **Ups And Downs** ● **In Spain** ● **Neverland**

((Flawless power-pop. Sources tapped include Big Star, Beatles, Beach Boys, Byrds, et al., but the music is never derivative. Reminiscent patterns flit in and out of the music but one can never quite pin them down. Paul Revere and the Raiders? Yardbirds? No, it's the dB's, choice leaders in original theft. Anti-fashion/pro-pop/subversive rhythms/crawling harmonies. If only others dared to follow. We'd be happy there. **))** – Ed.

Musicians: **Chris Stamey** (vocals, guitar) ● **Peter Holsapple** (vocals, guitar) ● **Gene Holder** (bass) ● **Will Rigby** (drums) ● and others

193

The Specials

'More Specials'

Label: **Two-Tone/ –**
Date: **1980**

Includes: **International Jet Set** ● **Stereotypes** ● **Enjoy Yourself** ● **Man At C&A** ● **Do Nothing** ● **Hey Little Rich Girl**

((Previously proud to instigate a bluebeat/ska revival, the Specials were now unashamed to announce the profound influence of hotel lift muzak. This contemporary cynicism was compounded by blatant political disgust, unexpurgated street logic and the brilliantly cheeky keyboards of Jerry Dammers. **))** – S.P.

((Polemic for the Eighties, awesomely anticipatory, Jamaican nihilism of the Sixties translocated to the shadow of Spaghetti Junction. **))** – S.L.

Musicians: **Jerry Dammers** (keyboards) ● **Neville Staples** (vocals) ● **Terry Hall** (vocals) ● **Lynval Golding** (guitar) ● **Roddy Radiation** (guitar) ● **John Bradbury** (drums) ● **Horace Gentleman** (bass)

194

Madness

'One Step Beyond'

Label: **Stiff/Stiff**
Date: **1979**

Includes: **One Step Beyond** ● **Bed And Breakfast Man** ● **Chipmunks Are Go!** ● **Night Boat To Cairo** ● **The Prince**

((Pop/Ska for youngsters everywhere. The

soundtrack to the witty, 'nutty' Madness cult symbolised by pork pie hats, Madness trains, number two brush haircuts and wonderfully controlled idiot dancing. **))** – **S.P.**

((Started as exact replica of mid-Sixties ska plus wacky stage visuals, became the wittiest pop eclecticism of the English Eighties, with even better visuals, courtesy the video revolution. **))** – **S.L.**

Musicians: **Mike Barson** (keyboards) • **Chris Foreman** (guitar) • **Graham 'Suggs' McPherson** (vocals) • **Mark Bedford** (bass) • **Lee Thompson** (sax) • **Woody Woodgate** (drums) • **Chas Smash** (vocals, fancy footwork)

195

Dexy's Midnight Runners

'Searching For The Young Soul Rebels'

Label: **Parlophone/–**
Date: **1980**

Includes: **Burn It Down** • **Geno** • **I'm Just Looking** • **Keep It** • **I Couldn't Help If I Tried** • **Love Part One** • **There, There My Dear**

((Without the hit single 'Geno', this band might not have achieved so much so soon. But that track has many equals on this album, from the controlled fury of 'Burn It Down' through to the unison punch of 'There, There My Dear', the

parting shot from a soon to be dissolved line-up. A record that exudes power at any volume and proof that traditional values don't have to mean unexciting music. **))** – **M.H.**

Musicians: **Kevin Rowland** (vocals, guitar) • **Groek** (drums) • **Pete Williams** (bass) • **Jimmy Paterson** (horns) • **Steve Spooner** (horns) • **J.B.** (horns)

196

Roky Erickson And The Aliens

'The Evil One'

Label: **–/415 Records**
Date: **1981**

Includes: **Sputnik** • **Click Your Fingers Applauding The Play** • **If You Have Ghosts** • **Creature With The Atom Brain** • **Bloody Hammer** • **The Wind And More**

((The Thirteenth Floor Elevator singer returns from the asylum and mental torment with the greatest heavy rock album for years and years. Images of horror comics and grisly B-movies of the Fifties meet addictive riffs and the melodic psychedelic guitar style of Duane Aslaksen. This is heavy metal with a difference – (a) you can actually dance to it; (b) the lyrics are quite beautifully mad. Ex: 'It's not a hammer/It's not a chisel/It's not a chain buzz-saw/Of unlimited horror for Doctor O'Chane'. **))** – **Ed.**

Musicians: **Roky Erickson** (vocals, guitar) • **Duane Aslaksen** (guitar) • **Bill Miller** (electric autoharp) • **Fuzzy Furioso** (drums) • **Steven Morgan Burgess** (drums) • **Andre Lewis** (keyboards) • **Jeff Sutton** (drums) • **Stu Cook** (bass)

197

Alex Chilton

'Like Flies On Sherbert'

Label: **Aura/–**
Date: **1980**

Includes: **Rock Hard** • **Waltz Across Texas** • **Alligator Man** • **Boogie Shoes** • **Hey! Little Child** • **I've Had It**

(| Misunderstood and derided when it was released, *Like Flies . . .* should, with the passing years, be hailed as the classic it is. Alternating between scabrous wit and a jaded cynicism, this collection of psycho-billy, country-punk and rock trash leads the field in records that pose the age-old musical question: 'Rock 'n' roll? What Is That?'. **)|** – **Ed.**

Musicians: **Alex Chilton** (vocals, guitar) • **Jim Dickinson** (keyboards) • **Richard Rosebrough** (drums) • and others

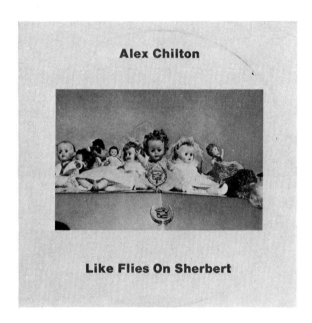

Alex Chilton

Like Flies On Sherbert

198

Lee Fardon
'The God Given Right'

Label: **Aura/–**
Date: **1982**

Includes: **Shoe Me (Like This Again)** • **When She Rains** • **Dreaming Still** • **Like An Automatic** • **Window Display** • **I Remember You**

(| The deep, full and sensual voice of someone like John Stewart is grafted on to songs not a million miles away from John Hiatt/Elvis Costello/Bruce Sprinsteen stuff. Okay, so it's derivative. Well, this is 1982, remember, and the world's natural resources of tunes and inspiration are fast running dry. Lee, if I am not mistaken, has actually just scraped the last 'angst' nugget from the 'singer-songwriter' reservoir – so enjoy it while you can. Byeeeeee!! **)|** – **Ed.**

Musicians: **Lee Fardon** (vocals, guitar) • **Jim Hall** (guitar) • **Jan Schelhaas** (keyboards) • **Colin Fardon** (bass) • **Chris Brown** (drums)

199

Haircut One Hundred
'Pelican West'

Label: **Arista/Arista**
Date: **1982**

Includes: **Lemon Fire Brigade** • **Love's Got Me In Triangles** • **Baked Beans**

(| At last – the welcome return of weeny-bop music. Adam Ant tried but by pouting too much, wearing too much make-up and making generally less than pleasant music, he came across like a cross between Steve Priest of Sweet and Les McKeown of the Rollers. Human League tried it, but by not smiling enough, and by having only one half-way decent tune, they came across like a surly, washed-up Abba. Haircut One Hundred make no such mistakes. Gorgeous tunes, tender smiles, and a genuine love of tractors makes them the Monkees of the Eighties. **)|** – **Ed.**

Musicians: **Nick Heyward** (vocals, guitar) • **Graham Jones** (guitar) • **Les Nemes** (bass) • **Mark Fox** (congas) • **Phil Smith** (sax) • **Blair Cunningham** (drums)

200

"The future is in your hands . . ."

Ten: Ninety-Nine Essential Pop Singles

1 **Abba:** S.O.S. (1975)
2 **Annette:** The Monkey's Uncle (1965)
3 **P. P. Arnold:** The First Cut Is The Deepest (1967)
4 **B-52's:** Rock Lobster (1978)
5 **Barbarians:** Moulty (1966)
6 **Beatles:** Paperback Writer (1966)
7 **Blue Oyster Cult:** (Don't Fear) The Reaper (1976)
8 **David Bowie:** Heroes (1977)
9 **Box Tops:** 'You Keep Tightening Up On Me (1970)
10 **Buzzcocks:** Ever Fallen In Love (1979)
11 **Byrds:** Eight Miles High (1965)
12 **Susan Cadogan:** Hurt So Good (1975)
13 **Castaways:** A Man's Gotta Be A Man (1965)
14 **Chantays:** Pipeline (1963)
15 **Alex Chilton:** Bangkok (1978)

16 **Clash:** Complete Control (1978)
17 **Contours:** First I Look At The Purse (1965)
18 **Craig:** I Must Be Mad (1966)
19 **Creation:** Making Time (1966)
20 **Cure:** Primary (1981)
21 **Dakotas:** The Cruel Sea (1963)
22 **Billie Davis:** Angel Of The Morning (1969)
23 **Bob Dylan:** Maggie's Farm (1965)
24 **Easybeats:** Friday On My Mind (1967)
25 **Eddie And The Hot Rods:** Do Anything You Wanna Do (1977)
26 **Electric Prunes:** Get Me To The World On Time (1967)
27 **Everly Brothers:** The Price Of Love (1965)
28 **Flamin' Groovies:** Shake Some Action (1977)
29 **Fleetwood Mac:** Green Manalishi (1970)
30 **Four Tops:** Bernadette (1967)
31 **Bobby Fuller Four:** I Fought The Law (1966)
32 **Glitter Band:** The Tears I Cried (1975)
33 **Richard Harris:** Macarthur Park (1968)
34 **Richard Hell And The Voidois:** Blank Generation (1977)
35 **Hello:** New York Groove (1975)
36 **Jimi Hendrix:** Burning Of The Midnight Lamp (1967)
37 **Jagged Edge:** You Can't Keep A Good Man Down (1966)
38 **Tommy James And The Shondells:** Crimson And Clover (1968)
39 **Kasenetz Katz Singing Orchestral Circus:** Quick Joey Small (1968)
40 **Kingsmen:** Louie Louie (1963)
41 **Kinks:** All Day And All Of The Night (1964)
42 **Billy J Kramer And The Dakotas:** Little Children (1964)
43 **Leaves:** Too Many People (1965)
44 **John Lennon:** Cold Turkey (1969)
45 **Love:** 7 & 7 Is (1966)
47 **McCoys:** Hang On Sloopy (1965)
48 **Merseys:** Sorrow (1966)
49 **Mindbenders:** A Groovy Kind Of Love (1966)
50 **Monkees:** Valleri (1968)
51 **Move:** Fire Brigade (1968)
52 **Music Machine:** Talk Talk (1966)
53 **Nazz:** Open My Eyes (1969)
54 **Ohio Express:** Chewy Chewy (1968)
55 **Freda Payne:** Band Of Gold (1970)
56 **Ann Peebles:** I Can't Stand The Rain (1974)
57 **Tom Petty And The Heartbreakers:** American Girl (1977)
58 **Elvis Presley:** Return To Sender (1962)
59 **P. J. Proby:** I Can't Make It Alone (1966)

60 **Public Image:** Public Image (1978)
61 **? And The Mysterians:** 96 Tears (1966)
62 **Ramones:** Don't Come Close (1978)
63 **Raspberries:** Overnight Sensation (1974)
64 **Paul Revere And The Raiders:** Him Or Me (What's It Gonna Be) (1967)
65 **Smokey Robinson And The Miracles:** Tears Of A Clown (1970)
66 **Tommy Roe:** Dizzy (1969)
67 **Kenny Rogers And The First Edition:** Ruby Don't Take Your Love To Town (1969)
68 **Ronettes:** Baby I Love You (1963)
69 **Tim Rose:** Morning Dew (1967)
70 **Todd Rundgren:** I Saw The Light (1972)
71 **Searchers:** Needles And Pins (1965)
72 **Seeds:** Can't Seem To Make You Mine (1966)
73 **Shangri-Las:** Remember (Walkin' In The Sand) (1964)
74 **Jackie De Shannon:** When You Walk In The Room (1963)
75 **Sir Douglas Quintet:** Dynamite Woman (1969)
76 **Small Faces:** Afterglow (1969)
77 **Soft Boys:** (I Want To Be An) Anglepoise Lamp (1978)
78 **Sonny:** Laugh At Me (1965)
79 **Sorrows:** Take A Heart (1965)
80 **Spirit:** 1984 (1970)
81 **Dusty Springfield:** Going Back (1966)
82 **Standells:** Dirty Water (1966)
83 **Status Quo:** Whatever You Want (1979)
84 **Strangeloves:** Nigh Nite (1966)
85 **Strawberry Alarm Clock:** Incense And Peppermints (1967)
86 **Supremes:** Nathan Jones (1971)
87 **Syndicate Of Sound:** Little Girl (1966)
88 **Table:** Do The Standing Still (Classics Illustrated) (1977)
89 **Sharon Tandy:** Stay With Me (1967)
90 **Television:** Little Johnny Jewel (1967)
91 **Troggs:** Wild Thing (1966)
92 **Turtles:** Happy Together (1967)
93 **Vanilla Fudge:** You Keep Me Hanging On (1967)
94 **Walker Brothers:** The Electrician (1978)
95 **Who:** I Can't Explain (1965)
96 **Betty Wright:** Clean Up Woman (1971)
97 **Yardbirds:** Happenings Ten Years Ago (196)
98 **Neil Young:** Cinnamon Girl (1970)
99 **Warren Zevon:** Werewolves Of London (1978)